W9-AOL-823

Experimenting with
Physics

John Farndon

Marshall Cavendish
Benchmark
New York

Marshall Cavendish Benchmark
99 White Plains Road
Tarrytown, New York 10591
www.marshallcavendish.us

Library of Congress Cataloging-in-Publication Data

Farndon, John.
  Experimenting with physics / by John Farndon. – 1st ed.
    p. cm. – (Experimenting with science)
  Summary: "Explores and explains physics concepts—including energy, motion, simple machines, gravity, flight, electricity, and magnetism—and provides experiments to aid in understanding physics"—Provided by publisher.
  Includes index.
  ISBN 978-0-7614-3929-5
  1. Physics—Juvenile literature.   2. Physics—Experiments—Juvenile literature.   I. Title.
  QC25.F34 2009
  530.078–dc22

                                        2008017568

Cover design by Virginia Pope
The photographs in this book are used by permission and through the courtesy of:
Shutterstock: front cover, back cover, 1, 3; gary718, 6, 7; Marianne de Jong, 8; Tomasz Trojanowski, 9 (inset); Dmitry Yashkin, 12 (inset); Archetype, 13; PhotoCreate, 16, 96; Dhoxax, 17; Chen Wei Seng, 18; Kalim, 22; Marcio Eugenio, 26; Amy Myers, 28; jkitan, 32; Avesun, 36; Le Loft 1911, 38; Vladmir Sazonov, 40 (inset); ORKO, 42; David Woods, 47; Tamara Kulikova, 55 (inset); Sergey I, 57; Hywit Dimyadi, 61; Gary Fowler, 63; Dmitry Kosterev, 64; Stephen Strathdee, 67; Douglas Knight, 69; Charles Shapiro, 70; Sally Scott, 83; Maciej Walczak, 84; Filipp Bezlutskiy, 91; Sergey Chushkin, 92; James Steidl, 95; Petra Roeder, 98; Rade Kovac, 99 (inset); Oralleff, 105. **Marshall Cavendish:** photographs by Martin Norris, 9, 10, 11, 12, 14, 15, 20, 21, 24, 25, 30, 31, 34, 35, 40, 41, 44, 45, 48, 49, 55, 56, 59, 60, 65, 66, 71, 72, 75, 76, 78, 79, 81-82, 85, 86, 89, 90, 93, 94, 99, 100, 103, 104, 107, 108.

Printed in Malaysia

1 2 3 4 5 6

Contents

What Is Physics?

What makes things move? How do they keep moving? What is gravity? How can things fly? At a basic level, physics is the study of matter and energy. Everything around us is made up of matter and all processes require energy. Every action you take—from throwing a ball to simply staying upright when you walk—involves physics.

Gravity is one physics concept that is easy to see. Drop an object and it falls to the ground. That is gravity at work. Notice that when you walk and move around you do not float off into outer space. Most people know that gravity keeps us on the ground. But have you ever wondered why, if the Earth exerts such a huge gravitational pull on us, we don't go crashing through the ground straight to the center of the planet? The answer has to do with understanding forces. At the same time that we are pressing down on the ground, the ground is pushing up on us with an equal and opposite force. Simple experiments can help us see these physics concepts in action.

Many physics concepts are related to each other, such as force, energy, motion, and work. How do force, energy, and motion cause work to be done? And how are we able to accomplish a lot of this work? The answer is: simple machines. These objects—such as a lever, pulley, and wheel—use physics concepts to help us reduce the amount of energy needed to do something. Creating simple machines and using them is not hard to do. You may not even realize it, but you are constantly using simple machines to complete daily tasks.

The science experiments in this book will help you understand these physics concepts—and many more. So, the next time you watch a plane take flight, you will have a better appreciation of how it is able to soar through the air. Or, the next time you use a screwdriver or ride a bike, you will see how simple machines make everyday actions so much easier. Through some careful thought and a little experimentation, you can see and understand how physics concepts affect you in every way.

From the wheel and axle of a ferris wheel to the centrifugal force that moves the swings, a carnival is a good place to observe physics in action.

Energy

Energy is one of the most important things in the universe. Without energy, nothing would happen, anywhere, at any time. Energy is involved in every movement in the universe, from the whirling of a huge galaxy to the tiny vibrations of an atom. Energy fuels the stars and keeps them shining brightly.

Down on Earth, energy lights our cities. It powers cars, trains, planes, and boats. It keeps factories going. It makes plants grow and fruit ripen. It keeps homes warm, and cooks food. It makes music, pictures on the television, and moving games on a computer. Every living body from bacteria to humans is kept going by energy.

Scientists define energy simply as the "capacity to do work." Work is really another word for making something change. So energy is the power to change something—typically by heating it up or making it move. Water is changed to steam when it is heated up, for example; the heat is energy.

Energy comes in many forms. Heat is a form of energy, called thermal energy. Light is a form of energy, too, called radiant energy. Electricity is also energy. Mechanical energy is the energy of physical movement, like a person running or machine turning. Chemical energy is the energy stored within chemicals. Other forms of energy include solar energy (the Sun's energy) and nuclear energy (the energy of atoms).

The bright lights, moving cars and buses, and heat of the city use huge amounts of energy.

KINDS OF ENERGY

Energy is the power to make things happen. It can exist in two ways. It can be ready to make something happen. This is called stored, or potential, energy. Or it can actually be making something happen. This is called kinetic energy.

Whenever something happens, movement is involved. This is why kinetic energy is also called movement energy. It is the energy something has when it is moving. A moving bicycle has kinetic energy. So does a ball whizzing across the football field, or a speeding bullet, or a plummeting rock.

It is clear that a moving object has energy because of what happens when something gets

A runner's body is a powerhouse of potential energy, stored as chemicals in the muscles. The body converts this energy to kinetic, or movement, energy.

Did you know?

The human body might not seem that efficient at converting its stored energy to action. Yet a person could ride a bike for half an hour on the chemical energy stored in one candy bar. It takes the energy of 2,000 candy bars to heat up a pot of coffee!

in its way. The painful impact if someone is hit by a flying ball, a bicycle or, worse still, a bullet shows this energy dramatically.

The more massive an object is and the faster it is moving, the more kinetic energy it has. In fact, scientists have found there is a way of calculating kinetic energy. They simply halve the object's mass (its weight) and multiply this by its velocity, or speed, twice. This can be written as an equation:

$$E = \tfrac{1}{2}mv^2$$

Here m is the mass of the object, and v^2 is its speed multiplied by itself.

Stored or potential energy is less easy to appreciate. A stretched elastic band or a squeezed spring, for instance, have potential energy because they will spring back—and move—as soon as they're let go.

A ball held above the ground has potential energy, too, because it falls if let go. Once falling, the potential energy becomes kinetic energy. The ball held high has energy because it is affected by Earth's gravity. The higher it is held, the more strongly gravity pulls, and the greater potential energy the ball has. Anything high up and in a position to fall has this potential energy. Because it depends on gravity, this energy is called gravitational potential energy.

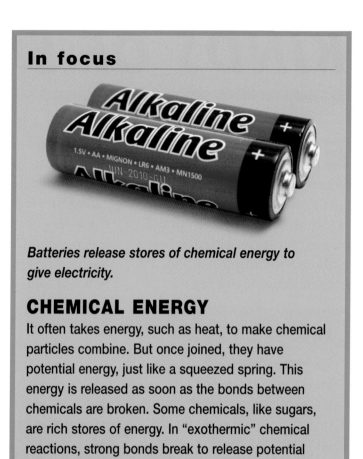

In focus

Batteries release stores of chemical energy to give electricity.

CHEMICAL ENERGY

It often takes energy, such as heat, to make chemical particles combine. But once joined, they have potential energy, just like a squeezed spring. This energy is released as soon as the bonds between chemicals are broken. Some chemicals, like sugars, are rich stores of energy. In "exothermic" chemical reactions, strong bonds break to release potential energy as heat. "Endothermic" reactions work the other way—taking heat from the surroundings to build strong bonds that are rich in potential energy.

With all these examples—the elastic band, spring, and ball— the potential energy does not come from nowhere. Energy has to be used to stretch the elastic band, squeeze the spring, and lift the ball. In fact, the amount of potential energy each gains is in direct proportion to the energy put in. The harder the band is stretched, the stronger the spring is squeezed, the higher the ball is lifted, the more potential energy each gains.

STORED ENERGY

You will need

- ✔ A trampoline of some kind, or simply a strong mattress you can safely jump on
- ✔ Yourself or a friend to jump on the trampoline

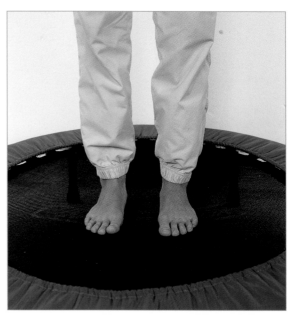

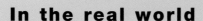

In the real world

ARCHERY

Archery depends on the buildup of potential energy in the bow's string as the archer pulls it back. When ready to fire, the archer lets the string go, and this energy is converted to kinetic energy in the arrow.

By pulling back slowly, an archer puts great potential energy in the bowstring.

1 Stand on the trampoline. There is no energy but the potential energy stored in your muscles.

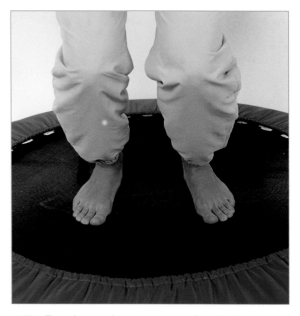

2 Bend your knees, preparing to jump and begin to use muscle energy.

What is happening?

Bouncing on a trampoline involves a constant switching between stored, potential energy (PE) and kinetic, movement energy (KE). Chemical PE in your muscles is converted to KE as you leap up. At the top of your leap, the PE due to gravity pulls you down, giving you KE. As you hit the trampoline, the KE changes to PE in the trampoline as it stretches. This is given back to you as KE as you fly up again, aided by PE from your muscles.

3 Jump high into the air. The muscle energy you used to launch you is now converted to kinetic (movement) energy.

Keep on jumping up and down on the trampoline. You should find that as you go on jumping, you need less and less effort to jump—or you can jump much higher with the same effort. This is because each time you fall and hit the trampoline, the trampoline stretches down a little, because it is made of elastic material. It then bounces back, giving you a lift on the way. The higher you jump, the harder you hit the trampoline as you come down, and the more it stretches—and so the bigger the push it gives you on your way back up.

MOVEMENT ENERGY

You will need

✔ A simple swing, either with a seat or a rope with a knot

✔ Yourself, and perhaps a friend to push you

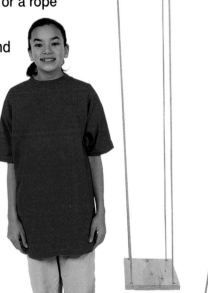

1 Sitting still on a swing, the only energy is potential—chemical in your muscles and gravitational from your weight.

What is happening?

To get a swing going, you use stored chemical energy in your muscles, swinging high to gain potential energy (PE) due to gravity. At the top of each swing, you have maximum PE. As you swing down, you lose PE, but gain kinetic, movement, energy (KE) as you move faster. The KE carries you up the other side. As you swing higher, you slow as KE is lost fighting gravity. Eventually all KE is gone, but you have gained PE from your height so you swing down, gaining KE again. So KE and PE alternate.

2 Bend your legs and start to swing back, by shifting your upper body weight forward.

3 Let yourself swing down by leaning back to shift your weight again.

In the real world

ENERGY IN SPORTS

A sportsman uses stored, chemical energy from his muscles, but he learns to exploit gravitational potential energy (GPE) and kinetic energy. A cyclist can save on muscle energy by using GPE to speed him downhill, and KE on the flat.

Cyclists need high energy drinks to supply muscles.

5 Near the top of the swing, pull your upper body forward sharply and curl your legs under again.

Keep on repeating this sequence, swinging forward and backward to build up momentum. You will have to put quite a bit of effort in to start with—shifting your weight in an S-shape from head to toe and back again. But after a while you should be able to swing fast and freely with little effort.

4 As you pass the lowest point, lean back and stretch out your legs to help pull you forward.

ENERGY CHANGES

Energy comes in many forms, but it always works in two ways—energy transfer and energy conversion. Together these are called energy transformations.

Energy transfer simply means it moves from one place to another, as when smoke rises or a person kicks a ball. Energy conversion means changing from one form of energy to another. A dancer's muscles, for instance, convert chemical energy into movement.

Natural transformations are happening throughout the universe all the time, and they keep the universe going. But people also rely on energy transformations to give them energy in the right form.

Mechanical energy can be converted to electrical energy by generators. As electricity, the energy is controllable, concentrated power for everything from trains to computers. Transformations ensure the energy is stored and delivered at the right time. A battery stores energy in chemical form then transforms it to electricity when needed.

It is not always possible to control when energy is transformed. An accidental explosion is the sudden transformation of chemical energy to heat energy.

Leaves are flat and wide to soak up as much energy from the Sun as they can. They use a green chemical called chlorophyll to convert this energy to sugar.

Did you know?

The leaves of plants are solar energy cells. They use sunlight to chemically join carbon dioxide gas from the air with water to make the energy-rich sugars plants need to grow. This process is called photosynthesis.

PUTTING ENERGY TO WORK

You will need

- ✔ A 12-inch (30 cm) length of ⅛-inch (0.3 cm) copper tubing
- ✔ A craft knife
- ✔ Pliers or vise
- ✔ A pencil
- ✔ A tealight candle
- ✔ A rectangular piece of balsa wood, cut into a boat shape

1 Ask an adult to grip one end of the tube in a vise or pliers, then gradually bend the tube into a coil around a pencil.

In the real world

STEAM LOCOMOTIVES

Steam locomotives work by turning heat energy to mechanical energy. They burn coal in a firebox to heat up water in a boiler, making steam. The steam drives a piston to and fro; the piston turns the wheels via connecting rods and cranks.

Steam locomotives are heat engines.

2 Place the candle on the balsa. Push the two ends of the tube right through the candle and the boat.

3 Invert the boat, and bend the ends of the tube backward at about 45°. Clean the ends of the tube with a pin.

What is happening?

All engines work by converting one form of energy to another. Heat engines—powering everything from trucks to space rockets—use heat energy to drive mechanical movement. This boat is a simple form of heat engine. Here the heat source is the candle. The flame heats the water in the coil of the tube. The water gets so hot that it turns to steam. The steam swells out of the tube, pushing the boat forward. The steam condenses (turns to water), and more water is drawn back into the tube. The candle heats the water again, turning to steam and driving it from the tube. So the boat moves forward in a series of pulses.

Place one tube end with the opening up under the stream from a faucet and suck the other end like a straw to fill the tube with water. Hold the water in with your fingers while you push the whole boat underwater. Let the boat come up to the surface with the candle upward. Dab the candle dry, then ask an adult to light it. The boat should start to move slowly.

Motion

Like every movement in the universe, running and kicking follow the same basic laws of motion worked out by scientists over the centuries.

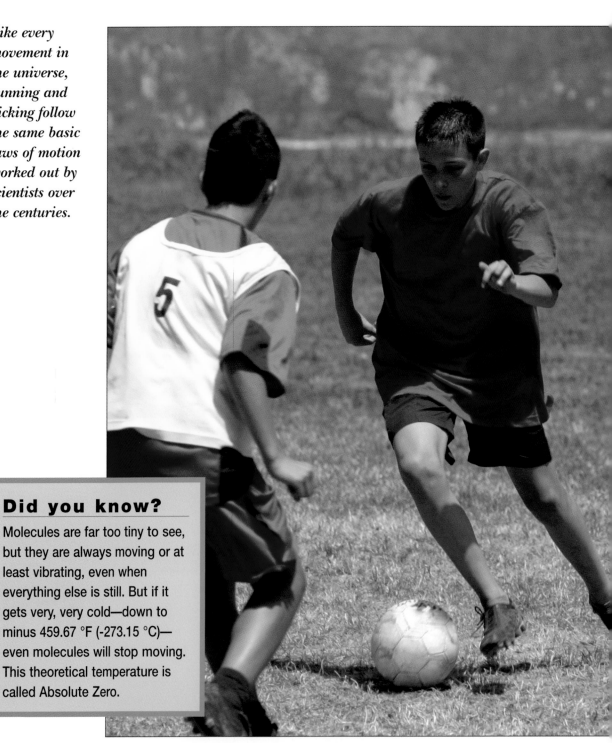

Did you know?

Molecules are far too tiny to see, but they are always moving or at least vibrating, even when everything else is still. But if it gets very, very cold—down to minus 459.67 °F (-273.15 °C)— even molecules will stop moving. This theoretical temperature is called Absolute Zero.

ANCIENT GREEK IDEAS

Movement was first studied scientifically by the Ancient Greeks, over 2,000 years ago. It was the Greek thinker Aristotle (384-322 B.C.E.)—once tutor to Alexander the Great—who discovered the key role of force. Aristotle realized that things only start to move when pushed or pulled by a force. What Aristotle could not see was how things like arrows keep moving without force. Aristotle could see that it takes the force of an ox to pull a plow and the force of a bow to fire an arrow. Yet the ox must keep pulling to keep the plow moving—the arrow flies on by itself. Aristotle's ideas were built on by other Greek thinkers such as Archimedes, but it was 1,700 years before English scientist Isaac Newton found the answer.

A statue of Archimedes.

Everything in the universe is moving. Some movement is really obvious, like a car speeding along a highway, or a ball bouncing on the pavement. Other movement is less noticeable, like the whirling of the earth beneath our feet or the vibration of tiny atoms.

Without movement nothing would ever happen. Over the centuries scientists have given a great deal of attention and effort to how and why things move. In fact, there is a whole branch of science devoted to the study of movement, called dynamics. Scientists have discovered that nearly all movement obeys the same basic laws. Only things smaller than atoms behave differently.

Scientists who study movement use the word "motion" because it has a particular meaning. Motion is the change in position and orientation of an object.

When an object changes position, it moves from one place to another. Scientists call this motion translational. The simplest movement of this kind is linear motion, which means the object moves in a straight line. Linear motion can describe anything from a train on a railroad track to a raindrop falling from the sky.

When an object changes orientation it swivels to face in a different direction. Scientists describe this kind of motion as rotational, or simply as rotation.

HOW FAST?

Some things move so slowly it looks to human eyes as if they are still. The world's continents, for example, drift very slowly around the earth's surface, like ice on a pond. Yet since they move just an inch or so a year, it is only possible to detect the movement with sensitive laser satellite trackers.

On the other hand, many other things move so fast it is equally hard to see them moving. Even at relatively low speeds, some fast moving objects can become a blur, like the spinning wheels on a bicycle or vibrating guitar strings. The fastest thing in the universe is light, which can

150 years ago, the fastest people traveled on land was about 25 mph (40 km/h) on horse. Now speeds ten times this fast are common.

travel 186,000 miles (300,000 km) in just a second, and reach us from the Sun in less than eight minutes.

There are two measures of how fast something is traveling: speed and velocity. With speed, the direction of movement is not important. A bicycle's speed is simply how fast it is moving; it does not matter which way it is moving. Scientists call a simple rate like this a scalar quantity. Velocity shows how fast something is traveling in a particular direction. This is said to be a vector quantity.

Both velocity and speed are usually measured in terms of how far something travels in a regular time period—how many miles in an hour (mph or miles per hour), how many feet in a second (f/s or feet per second), and so on. Mathematically, velocity is the distance traveled divided by the time.

In practice, velocity can be measured only over a certain time and distance, however short. The time and distance are called limits. Theoretically, however, limits can be reduced to zero. Scientists then talk of instantaneous velocity. This is how fast something is moving at one instant—the instant a runner breaks the tape, say. In this instant, of course, no time passes so no distance is traveled, however fast the movement.

In the real world

SPEED COMPARISONS

Fingernails grow	0.02 in (0.05 cm) per week
Bacteria slither	0.00001 mph (0.00016 km/h)
Snails slide	0.005 mph (0.008 km/h)
Tortoises crawl	0.17 mph (0.27 km/h)
Fastest human sprints	34.3 mph (54.9 km/h)
Cheetah runs	63 mph (100 km/h)
Peregrine falcon dives	217 mph (350 km/h)
Fastest road car	217 mph (350 km/h)
Fastest helicopter	249 mph (400 km/h)
Tornado whirls	281 mph (450 km/h)
Fastest boat	319.6 mph (514.4 km/h)
Fastest train	320 mph (515 km/h)
Fastest jet car on land	633.5 mph (1,019 km/h)
Sound travels	760 mph (1,220 km/h)
Land speed record	763 mph (1,228 km/h)
Fastest airliner	1,600 mph (2,587 km/h)
Fastest jet plane	4,520 mph (7,274 km/h)
Space shuttle	16,600 mph (26,715 km/h)
Fastest humans have traveled, aboard *Apollo 10*	24,791 mph (39,897 km/h)
Earth orbits the Sun	66,620 mph (107,210 km/h)

Did you know?

Light is the fastest thing in the universe, traveling 299,792,458 meters per second (about 186,000 miles per hour). In fact, because scientists can measure the speed of light more accurately than they can a meter, they define a meter as 1/299,792,458 of the distance light travels in a second. Remarkably, unlike anything else, light's speed is always the same, no matter how or where you measure it, so scientists refer to the speed of light as a constant. Recently, though, researchers in Australia suggested that light may be getting slightly slower as the universe gets older.

MEASURING SPEED

You will need

- ✔ A stopwatch
- ✔ A small ball of modeling clay
- ✔ A couple of small pencils use as markers)
- ✔ A ball
- ✔ A tape measure

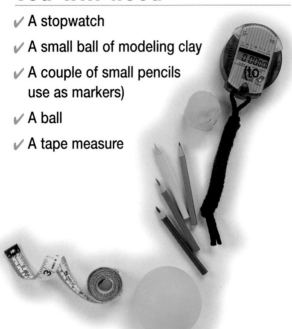

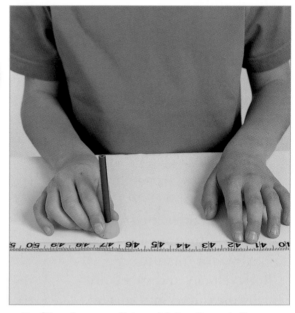

1 Stand a pencil in a blob of modeling clay to act as a marker. Measure out 10 ft (3 m) and set up another pencil.

What is happening?

The speed or velocity of a moving object can be worked out from the time it takes to travel a particular distance. In this experiment, the distance the ball travels is 10 ft (3m). If the ball takes 2 seconds to complete the course, its speed is 10 ft in 2 seconds. To make speed comparisons, however, you need to know how far the ball travels in a standard time, such as 1 second. To work this out, simply divide the distance by the number of seconds, here 2. 10 divided by 2 is 5, so the speed is 5 feet per second. In this way, you can easily compare the speed of the ball over different runs and different distances.

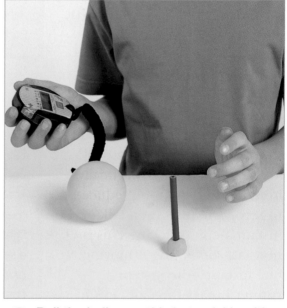

2 Roll the ball smoothly but quickly with one hand. Start the stopwatch just as it passes the marker pencil.

In the real world

SPEED GUNS

Speed guns were originally developed for the police to see if cars were speeding. Now they have been adapted to measure speeds in sport—from a baseball pitch to a tennis serve. They work by emitting radar waves and detecting them as they bounce back from the ball. The gun works out the speed from how much the returning waves are stretched or squeezed by the movement of the ball. This stretching or squeezing is called the Doppler effect, so the guns are sometimes called Doppler radar guns. Guns like these have shown that top male tennis stars like Mark Phillipousis serve at over 140 mph (230 km/h).

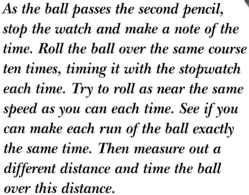

Women tennis stars serve at over 90 mph (150 km/h).

As the ball passes the second pencil, stop the watch and make a note of the time. Roll the ball over the same course ten times, timing it with the stopwatch each time. Try to roll as near the same speed as you can each time. See if you can make each run of the ball exactly the same time. Then measure out a different distance and time the ball over this distance.

GETTING FASTER

Few things keep moving at precisely the same speed for long. Nearly all moving objects slow down or speed up eventually. Positive acceleration is speeding up. Negative acceleration, or deceleration, is slowing down.

Acceleration is basically the change in speed over a particular time period. If the speed is measured in feet per second, the acceleration is how much that speed changes in each second—that is, feet per second per second. This can be written as feet per second squared, or ft/s^2.

Scientists describe acceleration as a change in

In order to take off, planes must accelerate to a certain speed in a short amount of time.

In focus

CALCULATING ACCELERATION

The change in velocity as things get faster or slow down is the difference between the final velocity (*v*) *and* the initial velocity (*u*)—that is, *v* minus *u*. The acceleration is how quickly this change in velocity happens. So the acceleration (*a*) is *v* minus *u* divided by the time (*t*), or:

$$a = (v - u)/t$$

If you know the initial velocity and the acceleration, you can work out how fast something is going after a certain time using this formula:

$$v = u + at$$

THROWING A BALL

Throwing a ball in the air means using muscle power to give it acceleration. When a ball is thrown in the air, the throw accelerates it upward, but gravity tries to accelerate it downward. The ball will only travel upward if the positive upward acceleration from the throw is more than the negative, downward acceleration of gravity. The ball falls back down as soon as the downward acceleration exceeds the upward.

A flying basketball is always balanced between the positive acceleration of the throw and the negative acceleration of gravity.

velocity rather than speed. Like velocity, acceleration is a vector quantity—that is, it always happens in a particular direction as well as at a particular rate.

Indeed, acceleration can simply be a change in direction, rather than a change in speed. All circular motion—from an orbiting planet to a spinning bicycle wheel—is acceleration. This is because the direction is always changing.

In most everyday events, the rate at which things accelerate is rarely steady. In a few situations, though, acceleration is constant —that is, the change in velocity and direction is unvarying. The best known example of constant acceleration is gravity. Gravity always makes things fall at the same rate and in the same direction: downward.

UNDERSTANDING ACCELERATION

You will need

- ✓ Several sheets of plain white paper
- ✓ A compass
- ✓ Food coloring or ink
- ✓ A small toy truck or car
- ✓ Scissors
- ✓ A stopwatch
- ✓ An empty soda bottle
- ✓ A plank of wood
- ✓ A tape measure

1 Cut the cone-shaped top off the soda bottle with scissors. The bottle top will be your ink reservoir.

In the real world

GRAVITY ACCELERATION

The earth's gravity accelerates things downward. The truck in this experiment is accelerated down the ramp by the pull of gravity. When things are falling freely, they all experience the same acceleration due to gravity, gaining speed at 32 ft per second per second (9.8 m/s^2). After falling 0.1 seconds, a ball would have fallen barely 2 inches and be falling just 3 ft per second. After falling for 0.3 seconds, it would have fallen 17 inches and reached 10 ft per second. After just 0.6 seconds, it has fallen 5 ft and reached 20 ft per second.

2 With an adult watching, make a very small hole in the bottle cap with the point of a compass.

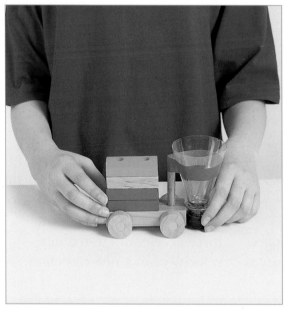

3
Tape the bottle top as upright as possible to the back of the toy truck, with the cap downward.

Cover the plank with paper. Hold your finger over the hole in the bottle cap, then pour a little food color or ink into the bottle top. With your finger still over the hole, set the truck at the top of the ramp, gently lifting to provide a very slight incline. Let the truck go, and watch the ink drops it leaves behind as it accelerates down the slope.

What is happening?

As something accelerates and travels faster, it covers a greater distance in each time period. Here, the drops of ink fall from the truck at a steady rate. Yet as the truck rolls down the slope, the ink drops get farther and farther apart, showing it is traveling farther and farther in the same time. This means it must be accelerating. This experiment is simple in theory, but it can be hard to make work well. The longer and more gentle the slope, the better it will work. Check that the cap drips ink evenly. Start with the hole too small, then enlarge it.

STARTING TO MOVE

Nothing moves of its own accord. Every object is said to have inertia, and only moves if it is forced to. If anything starts to move, it is because some force is pushing or pulling on it, overcoming its inertia.

Similarly, any moving object goes on moving for the same rate forever, in the same direction. It only varies its pace or direction if something forces it to slow down, speed up, or change course. This tendency to keep going at the same speed is called momentum. Momentum is what throws passengers forward when a car suddenly slams on its brakes.

Inertia and momentum mean there is never any change in an object's motion unless some force accelerates it to a new velocity or in a new direction.

Rollerbladers and skaters need much more muscle power to start moving. Once moving, their momentum helps keep them going with much less effort.

Did you know?

Momentum is mass times velocity. The standard science units for momentum are kilogram meters per second or kg.m/s. So a 1,000 kg car moving at 20 m/s would have a momentum of 20,000 kg.m/s. Momentum could also be measured in pound feet per second.

NEWTON'S LAWS OF MOTION

Isaac Newton (1643-1727) was one of the greatest scientists. In 1665, he worked out three laws of motion. These laws underpin modern science and are used to understand the motion of anything from atoms to galaxies. The First Law is about inertia and momentum, and says an object accelerates or slows down only when a force is applied. The Second Law says that the acceleration depends on mass and force—that is, how heavy the object is and how hard it is being pushed or pulled. The Third Law is about how forces interact. It says that when a force pushes or acts one way, an equal force pushes in the opposite direction.

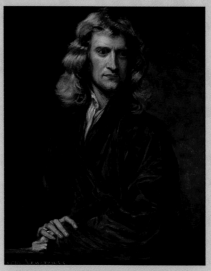

Newton's discoveries remain the foundation of science today.

The effect of a force on an object depends on the object's mass. Mass is how heavy something is—or more exactly, how much matter it contains.

For scientists, there is no real difference between something moving at a steady speed and something completely still. With both there is no change without a force. So they use the word inertia to describe the tendency of an object to resist a change in velocity, whether it is still or moving. An object's inertia depends on its mass alone. The greater its mass, the greater its inertia and the less effect a certain force has on its motion.

Momentum, however, only applies to moving objects. When something is moving, the force needed to change its motion depends not only on its mass but its velocity, too. The faster and heavier an object is, the greater its momentum, and so the less effect a certain force has on its motion. Momentum is defined as the mass of an object multiplied by its velocity.

When two objects collide, they keep the same combined momentum. Their combined mass times their combined velocity is always the same, even if the balance between them shifts. So whatever momentum one object loses in the collision, the other gains. If one marble hits another, for instance, it may slow down or stop, but as it does, it passes on some or all of its momentum to the other. This is called the conservation of linear momentum.

FORCE AND ACCELERATION

When a baseball player hits the ball, the force of the swinging bat accelerates the ball. The large mass of the bat compared to the lightness of the ball means the ball can often rocket away into the outfield at tremendous speeds.

An object's inertia means it won't start moving without a force acting on it. Nor will it go faster or slower, or change direction, without a force acting on it. The force may change the object's velocity or direction.

A force can be thought of as something that accelerates an object—a push or pull that makes it move faster or slower or veer off in a new direction.

The amount of acceleration that a force creates depends on two things: the size of the force, and the mass of the object. The larger the force, the greater the acceleration. Pushing twice as hard on the pedals of a bicycle, for example, doubles the

Did you know?

The standard units of force are newtons. One newton is the force needed to accelerate 1 kg by 1 m/s^2. Force used to be measured in poundals. A poundal is 0.1383 newtons, or the force needed to accelerate 1 lb by 1 ft/s^2.

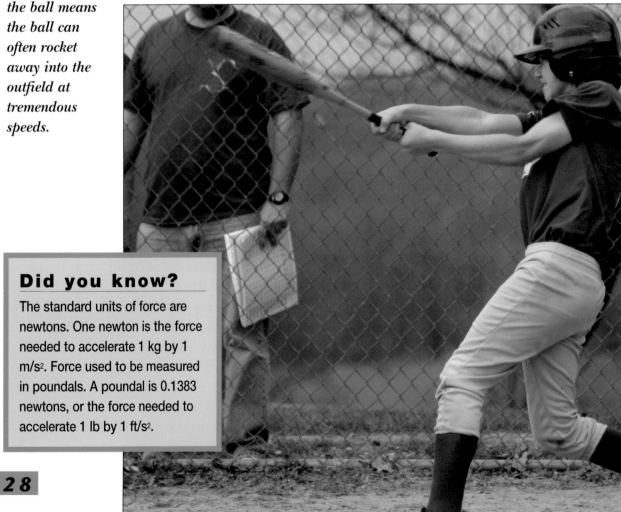

bicycle's acceleration. The acceleration is directly proportional to the force.

The effect of the force, however, varies according to the mass. A throw of the same force accelerates a light tennis ball much more than a heavy stone. To accelerate the stone at the same rate as the ball, it has to be thrown with much greater force. So acceleration is also directly proportional to mass.

Forces always act in a particular direction. If you throw a ball forward, the ball is accelerated forward. But objects are very rarely subjected to just

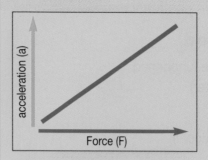
a single force. Usually, several forces act on an object, each pulling or pushing the object in a different direction.

The combined effect of these forces is called the resultant. The resultant is midway between all the forces. If one force pulls a bicycle to the left, and an equal force pulls it to the right, the bicycle goes straight on. But if the force pulling it to the left is stronger, the bicycle veers more to the left.

BEATING INERTIA

You will need

✔ A large soda bottle (unopened or refilled with water)

✔ Rubber bands

✔ Food coloring (optional)

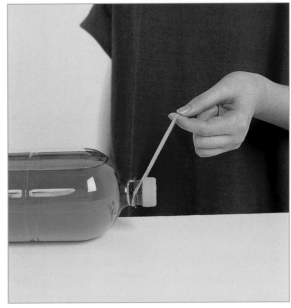

1 Place the bottle on a smooth, flat table. Loop the rubber band around the neck of the bottle. Apply glue if needed.

In the real world

WRECKING BALL

One of the most dramatic uses of momentum is the demolition or wrecking ball used to knock down concrete and brick buildings and other structures. A huge steel ball weighing up to 13,500 lbs (over 6,000 kg) is hung from the jib of a crane. The crane then swivels to swing the ball against the building. The huge weight of the wrecking ball means that it has tremendous momentum, even when swinging quite slowly. A long, fast swing can build up enough momentum to crash against the building with enough force to knock through solid concrete.

A wrecking ball demonstrates clearly the momentum of a heavy object when moving.

What is happening?

The stretching of the rubber band is a simple measure of how much force is needed to drag the bottle. The band is most stretched just before the bottle starts to move. This shows how a great deal of force is needed to overcome an object's inertia and get it moving. Once it is moving steadily, the band gets much shorter. This shows that much less force is needed to keep an object moving. This is because it now has momentum to keep it going. But to accelerate it, you have to apply a lot of force again, stretching the band once more.

2 Tug the band gently to drag the bottle. Keep pulling until it just starts to move. See how much the band stretches.

Keep pulling gently as the bottle gradually starts to move and continue to pull gently. Try to make the bottle move as smoothly and steadily as possible. Once it is moving evenly, look at how much the band is stretched. It should be much less stretched than when the bottle just started to move in Step 2 above. Now suddenly try to move the bottle faster. What happens to the band?

FRICTION

Not all forces make things move; some bring them to a halt. A moving object's momentum should mean it carries on moving at the same speed unless some force slows it down. Theoretically, it could go on moving forever.

Yet most things do slow down eventually. Nobody can throw a ball more than a few hundred feet, for instance. Nor has any body yet made a perpetual motion machine—a machine that goes on turning forever under its own momentum.

Racing cyclists try to cut friction with the air by wearing shiny clothes and streamlined helmets.

The reason is that forces slow things down. The main stopping force is friction. Friction is the force between two things rubbing together, and it occurs in almost every situation where things move.

When two solids rub together, jagged places on each surface catch together. These jagged places are clearly visible ridges and snags. But there are often microscopic jagged places even on apparently smooth surfaces. Sometimes the friction can be caused by the attraction between tiny molecules in each surface.

When a ball flies through the air, the friction is created by constant collisions between the ball and air molecules. The ball falls back to the ground as this friction slows it down enough for gravity to pull it down.

Friction tends to make things hot, because much of the energy of a moving object's momentum is converted into heat as the object slows down. Friction can also create noise, as the energy is turned into sounds, such as rubbing and scratching noises.

Sometimes friction is helpful. Without friction, people could not walk on the pavement without their feet sliding as if on ice. Friction makes car tires to grip the road. If tires didn't grip, cars could never brake or even turn corners.

Stopping distances from different speeds.

mph / km/h
15 / 24
20 / 32
25 / 40
30 / 48
40 / 64
50 / 80
55 / 88
60 / 96

0 ft   50 ft   100 ft   150 ft   200 ft   250 ft   300 ft

Driver's thinking time

CAR STOPPING DISTANCES

Cars rely on friction to slow down and stop. Their brakes slow the wheels using friction, with pads rubbing against discs on each wheel. The wheels slow the whole car down, relying on friction between the tires and the road. The distance needed to stop a car depends not only on the speed and weight of the car and the efficiency of its brakes, but also the condition of the road. It takes much longer to stop a car on a slippery, wet road than on a dry one.

Often, friction is a problem. It impairs the efficiency of car engines, turning motion into heat. It also makes it hard to slide a heavy object such as a washing machine across a floor.

The amount of friction between two surfaces depends on the two materials and how hard they are pushed together. The amount of friction between two materials is given a rating called the coefficient of friction. Rubber sliding on concrete has a coefficient of 0.8, which is high. Teflon sliding on steel is 0.04, which is very low.

ROUGH AND SMOOTH

You will need

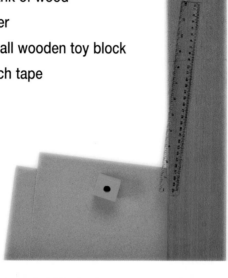

- ✓ A plank of wood
- ✓ A ruler
- ✓ A small wooden toy block
- ✓ Scotch tape

1 Place the toy block on the plank. Lift the plank up gradually until the block starts to slide down the slope.

In focus

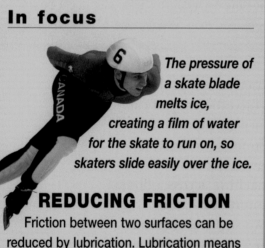

The pressure of a skate blade melts ice, creating a film of water for the skate to run on, so skaters slide easily over the ice.

REDUCING FRICTION

Friction between two surfaces can be reduced by lubrication. Lubrication means putting a substance such as oil or water between the two surfaces. This keeps the two surfaces very slightly apart, allowing them to slide over each other more easily. Ice is slippery because the top surface melts, creating a film of water that reduces friction.

2 Measure the height of the plank at the point where the block starts to slide.

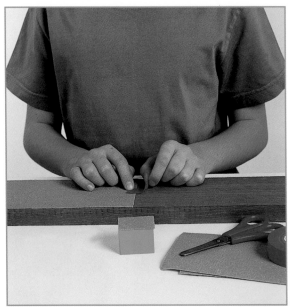

What is happening?

The greater the friction between two surfaces, the greater force is needed to overcome it and make the objects move. Because the block and plank are smooth, the friction between them is low. So, as the measurement in Step 2 shows, the toy block slides when the slope is gentle and the force of gravity pulling the block down the slope is weak. Putting sandpaper on each surface increases the friction. The grains of sand on each surface interlock and stop them sliding together. So the slope must be much steeper and the force of gravity greater to overcome the friction and make the block slide.

3 Stick sandpaper on the top side of the plank. Stick a small square of sandpaper to the toy block.

Place the toy block on the plank at the same point as in Step 2, with the sandpaper side facing down. Lift the plank up gradually until the block begins to slide down the slope. You may find the brick never slides, but simply tips over. Measure the height of the slope when the block just begins to slide or tip over.

Simple Machines

Even the most complicated machines usually incorporate one of five basic machines. Wheels and axles, for example, are a key component of every car.

Did you know?

The first known wheeled vehicles were wheeled sleds, as shown in ancient Sumerian pictures (from Uruk in modern Iraq) that date back to 3200 BC. And a pottery cup in the shape of a wheeled wagon was found in a grave in Szigetszentmarton in Hungary. This dates back to 2900 BC.

Wheels, levers, and pulleys are all machines—devices that make tasks easier for us to do. Some machines, such as screwdrivers, are simple. Others, such as washing machines and trucks, are much more complicated.

In the last 200 years, we have come to rely on a huge range of machines. Industries use giant presses, drills, boring machines, and lathes. Offices use computers, typewriters, and many other machines. Cars, buses, airplanes, and trains carry people around, while homes are full of machines from scissors to vacuum cleaners.

Some machines make it easier to move things—a door handle makes it easier to pull back the catch. Some machines move things that could not be moved in any other way, such as a dock crane that lifts a ship. When machines that move things are driven by natural energy such as wind, water, and coal, they are called "prime movers."

Some machines do not move things but instead turn one kind of energy into another. Refrigerators, for instance, use electrical energy to draw out heat and keep things cool.

There are five basic machines: the lever, the wheel and axle, the pulley, the wedge, and the screw. These simple machines can be used by themselves but

In the real world

Bows for firing arrows are among the most ancient machines, dating back at least 20,000 years.

THE FIRST MACHINES

Humans have used machines from the very earliest times. Among the most ancient machines is a little arm that some prehistoric hunters used to hurl stone-tipped spears with extra force. The bow and arrow is nearly as ancient and dates back tens of thousands of years. Cave paintings at La Marche in France show a horse's bridle dating back 17,000 years. But it was when people first settled down to farm around 10,000 years ago that a wide range of machines began to be developed, from plows to machines for milling corn.

are often combined to perform more complex tasks. Even the most elaborate machines usually incorporate at least one of them. A washing machine, for instance, will typically have a wheel and axle to turn the drum, a pulley to link the motor to the wheel, screws to hold it together, and levers to open the door—and even a wedge for the door catch.

LEVERS

A lever is a simple machine that makes it easier to move a load by amplifying, or making bigger, the effect of the effort used. When you use a spoon to pry the lid off a can or squeeze the handbrake on a bicycle, you are using levers.

Levers were the first machines, and have been used since prehistoric times. When Stone Age hunters strapped a bone handle onto their stone axes to make their blows more effective, they were making a lever. When early farmers used long sticks to lift stones from the ground or turn over the soil, they were also using levers.

The simplest levers are nothing more than long, rigid objects, such as steel rods or planks of wood. One point on the lever, however, must be

A wheelbarrow makes it easy to move heavy loads because it combines a lever with a wheel and axle. The effort is provided by the muscles lifting the handles, and the fulcrum is the wheel on the ground.

Did you know?

Levers are used throughout the natural world. In fact, the human body has its own levers. Virtually every moving bone in the skeleton uses the lever principle. Your forearm, for instance, is a lever, with the fulcrum at the elbow. The effort is the forearm muscles; the load is your forearm, plus whatever you are holding in your hand. In the case of your forearm, the effort lies between the load and fulcrum.

In focus

LOAD AND EFFORT

The effectiveness of a lever can be worked out by very simple sums. The farther the effort is from the fulcrum relative to the load, the more effective it is. In fact, the load you can move with a certain amount of effort varies in exact proportion to its distance along the lever from the fulcrum relative to the load. If the effort is three times as far from the fulcrum as the load, it is three times as effective—and so you need a third of the effort to move the load. If the effort is only twice as far from the fulcrum, it is only twice as effective.

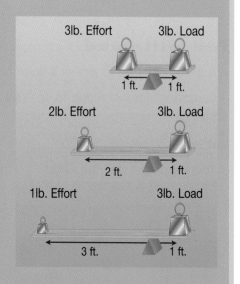

3lb. Effort   3lb. Load
1 ft.   1 ft.

2lb. Effort   3lb. Load
2 ft.   1 ft.

1lb. Effort   3lb. Load
3 ft.   1 ft.

The effectiveness of a lever depends on the relative positions of effort, load, and fulcrum.

fixed to act as a pivot. Scientists call this fixed pivot point the fulcrum. If the lever is a plank resting on a log, the log is the fulcrum. When you lever open the top of a can using a spoon handle, the rim of the can acts as the fulcrum.

When a force such as human muscle power is applied to one end of the lever, it moves a load placed somewhere else along the lever. Scientists call this force the effort.

Just how much effort it takes to move a load depends not only on the size of the load, but where on the lever it is applied. When the effort is a long way from the fulcrum, or the load is relatively close to the fulcrum, the effect of the effort is amplified—and so less effort is needed to move the load. When the effort is closer to the fulcrum, its effect is reduced and more effort is needed to move the load.

Because a lever is fixed at the fulcrum, the effort effectively turns the load in a circle. This is why the movement of a lever is called a turning effect (see page 22). Whenever you swing open a door, you make use of a turning effect—the hinge of the door acts as the fulcrum. The amount of force created by a turning effect is sometimes called the moment.

CLASSES OF LEVERS

You will need

- ✓ A plank of wood to act as a lever
- ✓ A shorter block of wood to act as a fulcrum
- ✓ Weights to provide a load
- ✓ Yourself to provide the effort

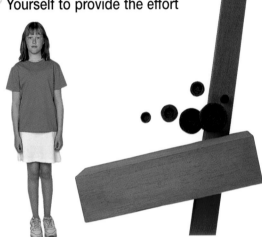

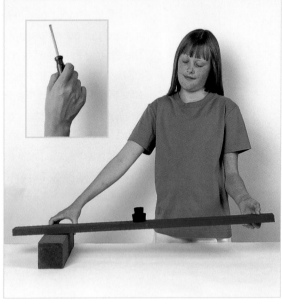

1 Rest the lever on the fulcrum, place the weights in the middle and lift the lever at the far end. This makes a Class 2 lever.

In the real world

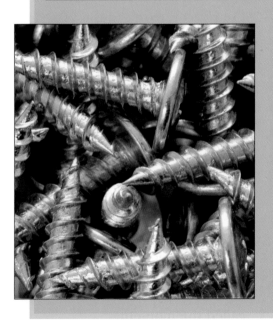

SCREWS

Screws are one of the five basic machines. They work by wrapping a groove around a shaft, in a very long spiral. This long groove means that the load—and so the work needed to push the screw in—is spread over a long distance. Screw threads are said to combine a lever—the screwdriver or spanner used to wind them in—with an "inclined plane." An inclined plane is a slope, like the sloping grooves on a screw, and is another simple machine; you need less effort to raise a load up an inclined plane than up a step.

Screws and bolts are ancient machines said to have been invented by Greek thinker Archytas in 400 BC.

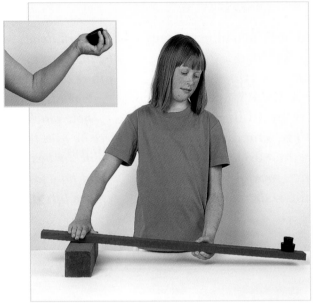

What is happening?

By swapping the places of the fulcrum, load, and effort on the lever, you are making three different Classes of lever. Class 1 levers, like scissors, have the fulcrum between the effort and the load. They are very effective but move the load in the opposite direction to the effort. Class 2 levers, like screwdrivers, have the load between the fulcrum and effort. Class 3 levers, like the forearm, have the effort between the fulcrum and the load.

2 Hold one end of the lever on the fulcrum, place the weights at the far end and lift it in the middle. This makes a Class 3 lever.

Rest the middle of the lever on the fulcrum, and place the weights on one end. Now try lifting the lever at the far end. You will find that the lever simply rises off the fulcrum and the weights don't move. If, however, you push down on the lever rather than lifting it, you will raise the weights easily, although you must take care to keep them balanced. This is a Class 1 lever. Now try lifting various weights with the three Classes of lever. Is one Class more effective than the others?

WORK AND EFFORT

In every machine, there are two main forces involved: load and effort. The load is the force to be overcome—that is, the force that is resisting movement. If a lever is lifting a stone, the load is the weight of the stone. The effort is the force used to move the load.

Machines work by cutting the effort needed to move a certain load. The amount a machine cuts effort is its mechanical advantage, or MA. To calculate the MA, scientists simply divide the load by the effort. When a machine gives MA it does not add energy. The total energy needed to move the load is always the same, with or without the machine. A machine works by spreading the

force needed. A machine typically moves a heavy load a short way by using a weak effort moving a long way. A 10-lb. load might be moved 1 ft. by a 1-lb. effort moving 10 ft. The distance moved by the effort divided by the distance moved by the load is called the velocity ratio, or VR.

The work done by the man in lifting the box depends on how much force he uses to lift the box, and how far he lifts it.

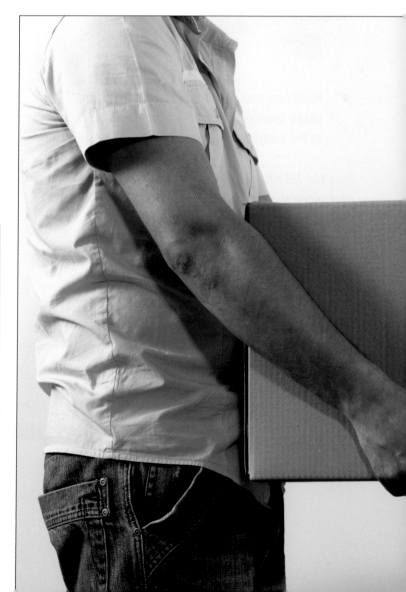

In focus

UNITS OF WORK

Scientists measure work in units of force and distance. In the United States, the unit is the foot-pound—the work done when a force of 1 pound moves an object 1 foot. In the metric system, the unit of work is the joule. This is the work done when a force of 1 newton moves something 1 meter. So a joule equals 1 newton-meter.

ARCHIMEDES'S MATH

The Ancient Greek scientist Archimedes was not the first to realize that machines make tasks easier, nor even the first to work out that a small effort can move a large load, if it is spread out over a long distance. But he was the first to prove it—and prove it mathematically. He also showed that work, effort, load and everything else can be predicted mathematically. This was the first time that math was used to understand the physical world, but it proved so successful that math is now the basis not just of all machine engineering but all advanced science.

In theory, the MA and VR should match. If a load is 10 times the effort, for instance, the effort must move 10 times as far. But no machine is perfect, since friction and other factors impair efficiency. So effort goes to waste and does not move the load as far as it should. In a machine that is only 50 percent efficient, a 1-lb. effort moving 10 ft. moves a 10-lb. load only 0.5 ft.— not 1 ft. as it should if it was 100 percent efficient. In fact, most complex machines are much less than 50 percent efficient.

Ultimately, what counts in a machine is how far the load moves, and the effort it costs to move it. Scientists call this the work done. Work is the force applied multiplied by the distance moved by the load.

WEIGHTLIFTING

You will need

✔ Three friends of nearly equal weight

✔ A seesaw

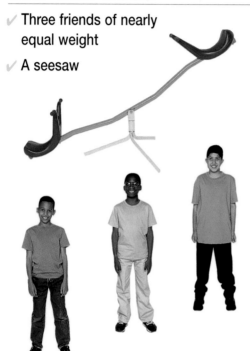

1 Two of you sit on the seesaw, one at each end. Try to achieve a level balance, with your feet off the ground.

In focus

WORK, LOAD, AND DISTANCE

Levers, such as seesaws, make work easier by reducing the force needed to move a load—by spreading it out over a greater distance. Mathematically, the work done equals the force times the distance. The amount of work needed to move a load is always the same, if the effect of friction is not taken into account. What can change is the distance. A small force can do the same work as a large force—and so move as heavy a load—if it works over a greater distance. In other words, the force must be farther from the fulcrum or pivot—or the load closer to it. With a seesaw, one person can balance two people or even lift them, simply by moving farther away from the pivot.

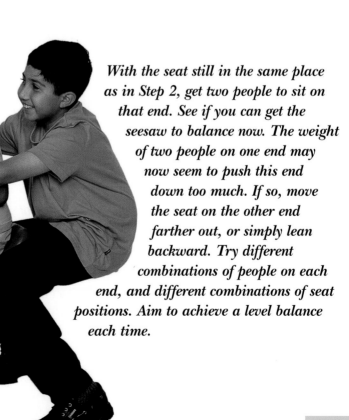

What is happening?

If two people sit on each end of a seesaw, equally far from the pivot in the center, they must be of equal weight to balance. However, if one moves nearer the center, the effect of his weight—his leverage—is reduced. So a person of equal weight at the far end lifts him high in the air, making it impossible to balance. Indeed, as the final step shows, one person can balance two other people of equal weight, if he is far enough from the pivot to give maximum leverage even if they are close to it.

2 Move one seat nearer the center, or let one person sit nearer the center. Now try to balance; you will find it difficult.

With the seat still in the same place as in Step 2, get two people to sit on that end. See if you can get the seesaw to balance now. The weight of two people on one end may now seem to push this end down too much. If so, move the seat on the other end farther out, or simply lean backward. Try different combinations of people on each end, and different combinations of seat positions. Aim to achieve a level balance each time.

WHEELS AND AXLES

Wheels are very rarely used by themselves. Instead, they are mounted on a shaft called an axle, which is attached to the middle, or hub, of the wheel. Sometimes the axle is fixed to the wheel and moves around with it; sometimes the axle goes through a hole in the wheel and the wheel turns around it.

The most obvious use of wheels and axles is on cars and trains, but there are many less obvious uses. Round door knobs are wheels and axles. So are faucets, the control knobs on a stereo system, and CDs when they are playing. In fact, almost every time something turns in a circle, there is likely to be a wheel and axle.

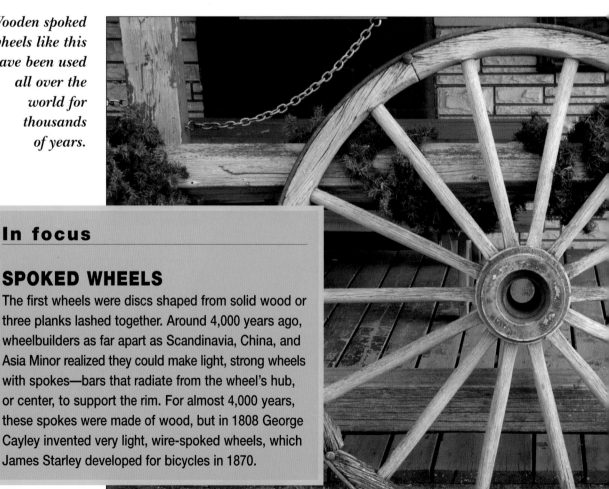

Wooden spoked wheels like this have been used all over the world for thousands of years.

In focus

SPOKED WHEELS

The first wheels were discs shaped from solid wood or three planks lashed together. Around 4,000 years ago, wheelbuilders as far apart as Scandinavia, China, and Asia Minor realized they could make light, strong wheels with spokes—bars that radiate from the wheel's hub, or center, to support the rim. For almost 4,000 years, these spokes were made of wood, but in 1808 George Cayley invented very light, wire-spoked wheels, which James Starley developed for bicycles in 1870.

A wheel and axle has many benefits. First, it makes it easy to achieve a smooth, continuous movement. Second, it enables someone to move something a long way while barely moving from the spot—imagine if all the grooves on an old long-playing record were stretched out in a long line.

Third, a wheel and axle is a lever—that is, a device that increases effective effort. Because the rim is some way from the hub, a force applied at the rim to turn the axle is

Did you know?

The gigantic Millennium Wheel was erected in London in the year 2000 to celebrate the millennium.

THE WORLD'S BIGGEST WHEEL

The biggest wheels are Ferris wheels—huge vertical wheels invented by American engineer George Ferris to carry people high in the air for the thrill of it. The world's biggest is the 500-ft. (150-m) tall Millennium Wheel, or London Eye, in London. It carries people around in 32 capsules to give them a spectacular view of the city. There are plans to build an even bigger wheel in France.

multiplied. The bigger the wheel is, the farther the rim is from the hub, and so the more the force is multiplied.

This lever effect is so useful that wheels and axles may first have been used simply to lift weights, for instance, to wind up buckets from wells. In these winding devices, or windlasses, there is an axle but no wheel. Instead, the axle is turned by a handle or crank.

BALL BEARINGS

You will need

- ✓ A couple of heavy books
- ✓ Some round (not hexagonal) pencils
- ✓ Small marbles of equal size
- ✓ Sugar cubes
- ✓ A flexible ruler (available at arts and crafts stores)

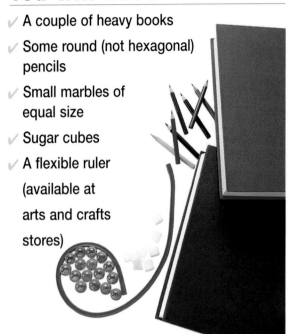

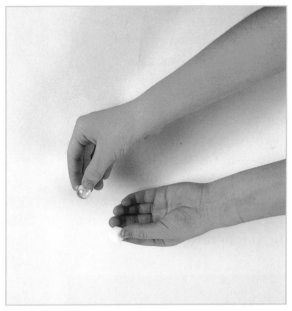

1 See how much farther a round object moves for the same effort by bowling a marble and sugar cube across a table.

In the real world

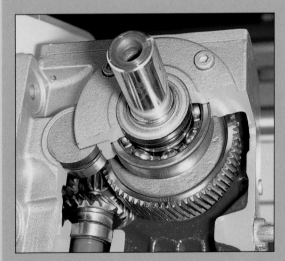

This cutaway view of a gearbox shows steel balls in a ball bearing around a drive shaft.

BALL BEARINGS

Where a part in a machine slides or rolls past another, it is usually supported by what is called a bearing. The bearing reduces rubbing that would sap power and also wear out the machine. A wheel needs a bearing at the place where it is mounted on an axle. On most early wheels, the bearing was just a collar of wood or leather lubricated with animal fat. Nowadays, most wheels are joined to axles by rolling bearings. Rolling bearings are made from hardened steel balls, rollers (cylinders), or cones that run in a circular groove around the axle.

2 Bend a flexible ruler to make a complete circle, then place about twelve identical-sized marbles inside the circle.

3 Carefully place two heavy books on top of the loop of marbles, then try sliding the books gently around the table.

What is happening?

With the marbles in a loop, you created a simple ball bearing, a device used in a huge range of machines to make it easier for things to move together. But, although you can swivel the books freely, you cannot move them far before they come off the bearings. Moving the books on the pencils shows how people made the first steps toward moving heavy things over a distance on wheeled transport, by placing sleds on rollers. The huge stones that were used to build monuments in the ancient world were probably moved this way.

Now try moving the books by placing them on round pencils instead. The books soon run off your pencil rollers, but, as each pencil comes out from behind the books, take it around to the front, so that the books slide on to it. In this way, you can move the books as far as you like.

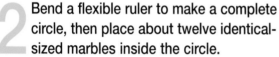

PULLEYS AND CRANES

For hoisting things straight up, the best simple machine is a pulley. This can be as simple as a rope flung over a bar. Pulling down on one end of the rope lifts a load tied to the other end of the rope. The task is made easier if the rope is run over a grooved wheel called a sheave, rather than a bar.

A single pulley does not cut the load; it works because pulling down is easier than lifting. A single pulley also means you can lift things high above your head, such as when hoisting a flag up a flagpole.

If it is free to move, however, a single pulley may cut the load as well. One end of the rope is fixed to a beam while the pulley is attached directly to the load.

Then, as the loose end of the rope is pulled up, the pulley moves with the load. This divides the load between the two halves of the rope, and so halves the effort needed to lift it—but the rope must be pulled twice as far.

Another way to cut the load is to combine pulleys—looping the rope first around one pulley, then others. This works by dividing the load between the strands of rope —the more strands there are, the more the load is cut. The load moves a shorter distance for each pull on the rope, but the lifting force is multiplied. Double, or even triple, pulleys are put into a system called a block and tackle. Here the pulleys are housed together inside a case called the block. The tackle is the rope.

In the real world

Cranes are machines that lift heavy objects with a pulley. In cranes called derricks, the pulley is attached to a long beam called a jib, or boom, and the pulley rope is usually wound in by a powerful motor. The biggest derricks are often mounted on floating barges to lift bridgework and salvage wrecks. The *Musashi* is a floating derrick crane built in Japan in 1974 that can lift over 3,000 tons.

SIMPLE PULLEYS

You will need

- ✓ A spring balance
- ✓ A long pole
- ✓ Length of rope
- ✓ A large bucket
- ✓ Water

1 Tie a rope to the balance. Hang a bucket of water from the balance hook and lift it by the rope. Check the weight.

In focus

HOW PULLEYS CUT THE LOAD

As with levers, pulley wheels cut a load by spreading it over a greater distance. A single pulley wheel can reduce the load if the rope is fixed at one end and the load hangs directly from the pulley so that the pulley moves with the load. Since both halves of the rope support the load equally, the load is split between them, so the force needed to pull the rope is halved. This system is said to give a mechanical advantage, or MA, of 2. But halving the load means halving the distance it moves, so for every two feet the rope is pulled the load is only lifted one foot. When there is more than one wheel, the MA equals the number of strands of rope. But each increase in the MA means a corresponding increase in the distance the rope must be pulled.

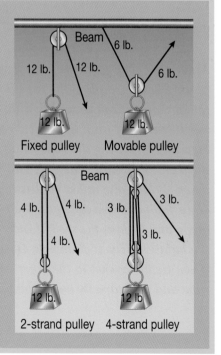

Fixed pulley   Movable pulley

2-strand pulley   4-strand pulley

What is happening?

Looping the rope over the bar creates a simple pulley. Lifting the bucket with the pulley is much easier than lifting it directly in the air. Yet, however you measure the weight, the load of the bucket is always the same. So this kind of pulley does not reduce the load. It simply makes lifting easier by allowing you to pull it from a better direction. To actually reduce the load, you need a movable pulley wheel or a system of interlinked pulley wheels.

2 Now find a fixed railing or set up a bar between two chairs to act as a pulley. Loop the rope over the bar.

Make sure your pulley is fixed firmly in place. Now try pulling the rope down to lift the bucket up. You should find this takes much less effort than lifting it directly, as in Step 1. Try pulling the rope at different angles—horizontally, at 45°, and straight down. Which one needs the least effort? Once you have decided, pull the rope at that angle and look at the weight indicated on the balance. Has it changed? Does it change if you tie the bucket to the other end of the rope and pull directly on the balance hook?

Gravity

Gravity is the force that keeps you on the ground. It also makes things fall and rivers run downhill. It is even the force that keeps the Moon close to the earth, and the earth and the other planets close to the Sun. It is gravity that holds together the earth and the Sun and the other planets, and keeps them from falling apart. In fact, gravity holds the entire Universe together.

Gravity, or "gravitation," is the universal force of attraction that tries to pull every particle of matter together. Every bit of matter in the Universe,

As soon as the bungee jumper leaps from the balloon's basket, the gravitational attraction between Earth and himself makes him plunge rapidly.

regardless of size, is said to exert its own "gravitational pull" on other bits of matter.

People sometimes talk about the earth's gravity or the Moon's gravity. But gravity is not the pull of one object, it is a mutual attraction—there is no pull unless there are at least two things pulling together. When a stone falls to Earth, it falls because the stone and the earth are pulled together by their mutual gravitational attraction. The stone moves, rather than the earth, simply because the earth has more mass.

Surprisingly, despite its universal importance, gravity is actually rather weak. We barely notice it as we walk around, lifting our feet against Earth's gravity with little effort. In fact, it is the weakest force in the Universe. It is effective only because there is so much matter.

Did you know?

It is hard to appreciate that gravity is a weak force, when you fall over hard and bruise your knees. But you hurt your knees because gravity is so much weaker than the forces that hold the ground together, which are called electromagnetic forces. If gravity were stronger than the electromagnetic forces, you would slip through the ground painlessly.

In the real world

NEWTON'S THEORY OF GRAVITY

At first, no one had any idea why things fall down or why planets circle the Sun. In 1665, a young man called Isaac Newton watched an apple fall from a tree to the ground. He wondered if the apple were not just falling but was actually being pulled toward the earth by an invisible force. From this simple but brilliant idea, he developed his theory of gravity, about a universal force that tries to pull all matter together.

FALLING FIRST

You will need

- ✔ A small stone
- ✔ A tomato
- ✔ Corks
- ✔ A rubber ball
- ✔ Sheets of paper
- ✔ A cutting board

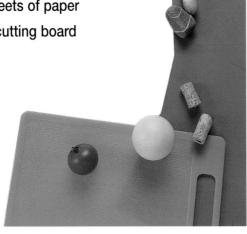

1 Hold two similar-sized objects of different weights, such as a stone and a tomato, in each hand, at exactly the same height.

In the real world

GALILEO AND THE TOWER OF PISA

The 17th-century Italian, Galileo Galilei, was one of the greatest scientists of all time. He was the first to use a telescope to gaze at the night sky and so discovered the moons of Jupiter. He was also the first to realize that gravity works by making things accelerate steadily and that everything falls at exactly the same speed, no matter how heavy it is. Common sense tells people that lighter things will fall slower, so, Galileo proved his idea with a famous demonstration, dropping lead shot balls of different sizes from Pisa's famous Leaning Tower.

The Leaning Tower in Pisa, where Galileo showed that everything falls at the same speed.

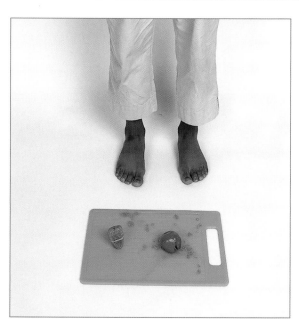

Objects dropped from the same height don't always hit the ground at the same time. Try dropping two sheets of paper at the same time. You may find that one flutters down more slowly than the other. Then try crushing one of the sheets into a tight ball. This will fall much faster.

2 Let the two objects drop at the same time onto the board. Listen out for which hits the ground first.

What is happening?

Like all forces, gravity makes things accelerate. So, if you drop something, it falls faster and faster toward the ground. But gravity makes everything accelerate downward at exactly the same rate, no matter how heavy it is. So, you hear the heavy stone hit the ground at exactly the same time as the much lighter tomato. However, a falling object may be slowed by the resistance of air. Compact, heavy objects like the stone and tomato are little affected by air resistance. But large, very light objects like a flat sheet of paper are. When the paper is bunched into a ball, the effect of air resistance is much less.

LIGHT AND HEAVY

The strength of the gravitational pull between two objects depends on their mass. Massive objects pull each other with great force; small, light objects pull toward each other with weaker force. The Moon and Earth pull toward each other with great force while an orange and a cherry only pull with little force—which is why their gravitational attraction does not pull them across a table toward each other.

People often use the word "weight" when talking about how heavy an object is. But scientists use the word "mass."

The bag of a balloon may be big, but it contains very little matter. Gravity pulls on the balloon so weakly that the balloon floats up into the air.

Mass is how much matter something contains. Every bit of matter has the same gravitational attraction. So, the gravitational pull between two objects depends on their mass—that is, how much matter they contain. This is always the same everywhere.

Scientists use the word weight to refer only to the force with which gravity pulls. In other words, the weight of an object is how hard it is pulled by gravity. This depends on where it is. Large planets are more massive than smaller planets and moons, so, gravity is more powerful there—everything there weighs more. If you were on the giant planet Jupiter, you would find it hard even to lift your arm. But on tiny Pluto, you could quite easily hurl a cow in the air.

In the real world

LIGHT AND HEAVY WEIGHTS

The smallest, lightest things in the Universe—those things with the least gravitational attraction—are tiny particles of light, called photons. Up the heavier end of the scale are dense ancient stars called neutron stars, and black holes in space which have a gravitational pull so powerful that they can suck in entire stars. In between, there are heavy things, such as the Sun, and lighter things, including sub-atomic particles called electrons. The Sun has about the same gravitational pull compared to an orange as an orange has compared to an electron.

Did you know?

An astronaut on the Moon has exactly the same mass as an astronaut on Earth. But because the Moon has much less mass than Earth, the pull of gravity there is much less. So, the astronaut weighs six times less on the Moon, which is why he can easily jump, even in a heavy space suit.

On the Moon, an astronaut is much lighter than on Earth.

FALLING FASTER

You will need

- ✔ A cardboard tube
- ✔ Some thin cardboard
- ✔ A tape measure
- ✔ Adhesive tape
- ✔ Large marbles
- ✔ A pencil
- ✔ Scissors

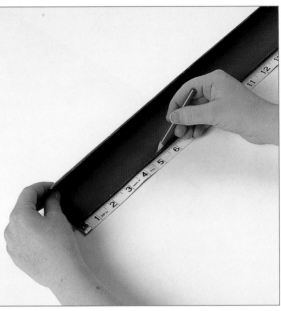

1 Cut the tube in half lengthways, and make marks every 6 inches (15 cm) along each edge. Cut a short slot at each mark.

In focus

When something falls straight down, gravity makes it accelerate toward the ground, getting steadily 32.16 feet (9.8 m) per second faster, every second that it falls. This steady acceleration is called the acceleration of free fall. As objects fall faster, however, the resistance of air has more effect. Eventually, air resistance balances the pull of gravity, and the object cannot fall any faster. From then on, it falls at the same speed. This speed is called the terminal velocity. An object's terminal velocity depends on its weight and shape, because both these factors affect air resistance. Compact, heavy objects have the highest terminal velocity.

2 Cut flaps from the cardboard in the shape shown. The curved section should match the inside of the half tube.

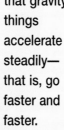

3 Slide the card flaps into the slots in the tube edges to make a series of gates. Slightly angle all the flaps the same way.

Hold the tube at an angle and release a marble from the top so that it runs down. The marble should just click through each gate without slowing down at all. If it sticks at any of the gates, adjust the flaps. Once the marble rolls smoothly through each gate, you are ready to start the test.

Release a marble, and listen carefully for the clicks as it passes through each gate. Are the clicks at exactly the same intervals, or do the intervals get shorter together as the marble rolls down? If you can't tell, try again with a shallower slope.

GRAVITY AT A DISTANCE

The power of the gravitational attraction between objects does not only depend on their mass. It also depends on the distance between them. The farther apart they are, the less the pull of gravity between them.

The Sun is so massive that the pull of its gravity can be felt over huge distances. This is why the earth and all the other planets keep circling it. Even so, its effect on small objects far away is quite small. On Earth, the effect of the Sun's gravity is generally negligible.

The pull of gravity is a balance between mass and distance. The bigger and heavier two things are, and the closer they are, the more strongly gravity pulls them

The Moon is far away, but massive enough for its gravity to be felt here on Earth.

Did you know?

The force of gravity varies slightly from place to place on Earth. It is stronger at the poles, for instance, than at the Equator, because the poles are very slightly closer to the center of the earth. For the same reason, Earth's gravity is more powerful at sea level than it is at the top of mountains. It is also more powerful above parts of the earth's rocky crust where there are especially dense rocks.

In focus

The power of gravity lessens as things get further apart. In fact, it gets weaker with the square of the distance—that is, the distance multiplied by the distance. This is called the inverse square law. So the greater the distance, the more it must be multiplied, which means the gravitational pull is very weak. The pull of gravity between two objects two miles apart is four times as weak—two times two—as two objects one mile apart.

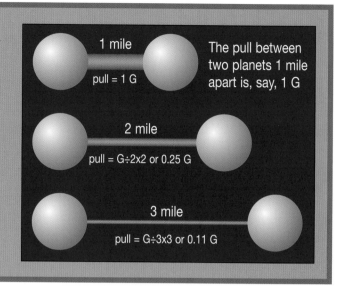

1 mile
pull = 1 G

The pull between two planets 1 mile apart is, say, 1 G

2 mile
pull = G÷2x2 or 0.25 G

3 mile
pull = G÷3x3 or 0.11 G

together. The smaller and lighter they are, and the farther apart, the more weakly gravity pulls them together.

In fact, the pulling power of gravity is always the same anywhere. It is considered a universal constant. The effect of the mass of two objects and the distance between them is the same everywhere.

The relationship between mass, distance and gravity is so precise that scientists can make all kinds of calculations about the Universe. They need only the mass of one star, for instance, to work out the mass of a nearby star, from the distance between them.

This kind of calculation has allowed scientists to do everything from plotting the course of a spacecraft to predicting where a new planet might be found.

INTO SPACE

Launching a spacecraft calls for massive rockets that provide the thrust to accelerate the spacecraft upward against the force of gravity.

To get into space, spacecraft have to overcome the tremendous force of gravity holding them on the ground.

Airplanes use the air flowing over their wings to fly, but air gets too thin to support an airplane little more than 18 miles (30 km) above the ground. So, spacecraft have to gain enough acceleration to beat gravity by sheer force. The only motors powerful enough to produce this kind of acceleration, or "thrust," are huge rocket motors.

Rockets burn fuel to create hot gases that expand to drive the rocket upward. But, to provide the thrust needed to launch a spacecraft, they need

Did you know?

Nowadays, all astronaut voyages into orbit above the earth are made in the space shuttle. Unlike other spacecraft, the shuttle can be launched again and again. Like all spacecraft, it is launched on the back of rockets but glides back to Earth and lands like a plane. Two booster rockets power it up to 30 miles (48 km) then fall away. A big single rocket drives it to 80 miles (130 km) up then falls away, and the shuttle's own engines put it into orbit 120 miles (190 km) up.

LAUNCH ROCKETS

Launch vehicles burn so much fuel so quickly that they are basically giant fuel tanks. The *Saturn V* which launched the spacecraft that carried astronauts to the Moon was over 350 feet (110 m) tall. Even bigger and more powerful was the Russian *Energia* rocket, which could deliver more than 3 million kg of thrust. Most of these big rockets are powered by liquid fuels. To burn properly, the fuel needs oxygen, so the rockets also have tanks for liquid oxygen. The liquid fuel and oxygen (LOX) mix in a space called the combustion chamber. Then an igniter sets them alight.

to burn fuel at an awesome rate. This amount of fuel, however, is needed only for the initial launch, not for the entire space flight.

Once the rocket is traveling fast enough and high enough, it no longer needs as much power to combat Earth's gravity. So, spacecraft are usually boosted into space by powerful "launch vehicles." These are rockets in three or four parts, or stages. The stages each fall away one by one, once the spacecraft reaches a certain height or speed.

To stay up in space, orbiting the earth, a spacecraft must accelerate until it is flying fast enough to avoid falling. To stay in orbit about 120 miles (190 km)

up, it needs to reach 5 miles (8 km) per second—that is, almost 18,000 mph (30,000 km/h). This speed is called the orbital velocity. Typically, when a rocket is launched, it gains 120 feet (40 m) per second every second that it climbs. Climbing at this rate, it reaches orbital velocity in nine minutes, at a height of 120 miles (190 km).

To escape Earth's gravity altogether and fly off into space, it needs to go almost half as fast again as the orbital velocity. The speed it needs to achieve this is called the escape velocity. For a spacecraft at a height of 120 miles (190 km), the escape velocity is 25,000 mph (42,000 km/h).

CENTRIFUGAL FORCE

You will need

- ✔ A plastic bucket
- ✔ Several pitchers of water

1 Find a plastic bucket with a good, strong handle. Pour in a few pitcherfuls of water.

2 Hold the base of the bucket and gently rotate it. See how the water swirls around in a circle.

3 Stand where you can safely splash water, and spin the bucket, keeping it level at arm's length. Does any water spill out?

CENTER OF GRAVITY

Gravity does not pull more on one part of an object than another, so, in effect, it pulls the object down as if all its weight were located in one point, which is called the center of gravity. When you balance something, you are placing its center of gravity directly above the base. The object topples if the center of gravity is off to one side.

A skater can balance on a skate point in an upright pirouette because her center of gravity is vertically above it.

Once you feel you can spin the bucket keeping it level without spilling water, try whirling it vertically around at arm's length, right over your head. Providing you whirl it fast enough, no water should spill out, even when the bucket is completely upside down.

What is happening?

The water seems to defy gravity by staying in the bucket even when it is tilted. In fact, gravity is still trying to accelerate the water downward. But the acceleration given by your arm is greater. Only the bucket keeps it from flying straight out. The tendency for an object to fly out like this when moving in a circle is wrongly called "centrifugal force," but there is no force involved. The water has the momentum to travel on in a straight line. The force is your arm holding onto the bucket and spinning it in a circle.

Flight

Aircraft are the fastest means of transportation. They can soar straight over obstacles, such as mountains and oceans. Airliners (large passenger planes) can fly at over 500 mph (800 km/h). Some fighter planes can reach 2,000 mph (3,200 km/h). A trip across the Atlantic Ocean once took many days by sea. Now, it takes less than seven hours by air.

As a result, aircraft have transformed the way people travel. Millions of people now fly regularly far across continents

Did you know?

The first powered aircraft had a steam engine. The airplane was a large model made by Englishmen William Henson and John Stringfellow in 1845. It probably made one short flight.

FLYING MILESTONES

1909 Louis Blériot flies across the English Channel.

1914 The world's first regular air passenger service begins in Florida.

1919 John Alcock and Arthur Whitten Brown make the first nonstop flight across the Atlantic.

1927 Charles Lindbergh makes the first solo flight across the Atlantic.

1933 Wiley Post flies round the world.

1947 Chuck Yeager flies faster than sound in the Bell X-1.

1952 The *Comet* is the first jet airliner in regular service.

for short business trips and vacations. Major airports, such as Chicago's O'Hare, see scores of passenger flights every day.

People dreamed of flying for thousands of years. As long ago as the 15th century, Leonardo da Vinci (1452–1519) came up with an idea for an ornithopter, a machine with wings flapped by muscle power. But it was never made. Then, in the early 1800s, British engineer Sir George Cayley built the first glider, an aircraft with wings but no engine. It was not until 1903 that the American Wright brothers, Orville and Wilbur, made the first controlled flight in an aircraft that had an engine for taking off and powering it through the air.

LIGHTER THAN AIR

Hot-air balloon flights last a couple of hours.

Airplanes rely on wings to lift them into the air, but the first successful flights were made without wings, in balloons. Balloons are lifted by a big bag of light gas. Because gas is lighter than air, the balloon floats up, just as a cork bobs up if you push it under water.

In 1783, the first balloon flights were made in France, in paper balloons made by the Montgolfier brothers. They filled the balloons with hot air

AIRSHIPS

The problem with balloons is that they simply float where the wind takes them. But in 1852, Frenchman Henri Giffard made a cigar-shaped gas balloon, powered it with a steam-driven propeller, and then added a rudder to make it "dirigible" (steerable). Later in the century, with petrol engines and rigid framed bags, dirigible balloons became airships—the first large aircraft. In the 1920s, large luxury airships carried people across the Atlantic in style. But a series of disastrous fires, caused by the inflammable hydrogen gas, made people realize that traveling by airships was far too dangerous.

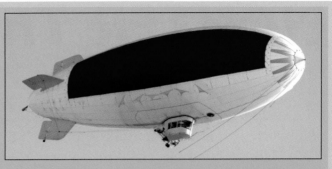

Newer airships are filled with helium gas, which is almost as light as hydrogen, but completely safe.

from a fire. Because hot air is less dense (lighter) than cool air, the balloons rose in the cooler air. One flight carried two men in a basket beneath.

A few months later, two other Frenchmen, Jacques Charles and M. Robert, made a different kind of balloon. They made a big bag from rubberized silk and filled it with hydrogen gas. Hydrogen is the lightest of all gases, so it lifted the balloon into the air.

Hydrogen-gas ballooning soon became popular because flights could last for several hours, unlike hot-air flights, which were over as soon as the air cooled. Gas balloonists could descend by using two control lines. One line let gas out through the top of the bag for going down. The other pulled open a "ripping seam" to let all the gas out once they were on the ground.

Hydrogen ballooning declined from 1900 when the first airplanes were made. People also realized how dangerous hydrogen is because it is inflammable, or likely to burst into flame. In the 1960s, however, Ed Yost, Tracy Barnes, and others in the U.S. began to experiment with hot-air balloons. Their balloons were made of nylon and filled with heated air made by burning propane gas from cylinders. The gas can be carried up with the balloon to replenish the hot air at any time. This proved so successful that hot-air ballooning is now a very popular hobby.

WARMING UP

You will need

- ✓ Two very large sheets of tissue paper
- ✓ A small hair dryer
- ✓ Paper glue
- ✓ Paper clips
- ✓ Scissors
- ✓ Cotton thread
- ✓ Thick paper or thin cardboard (for making the balloon basket)

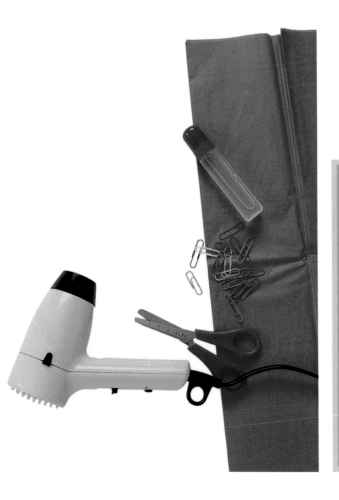

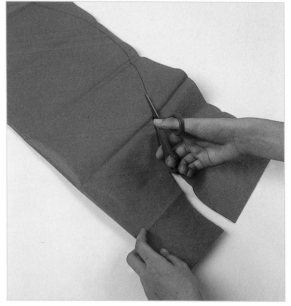

1 Lay the sheets of tissue paper together and fold in half lengthways. Draw a half balloon shape and cut through both sheets together to make two matching balloon shapes.

In the real world

THE FIRST MANNED FLIGHT

Throughout 1782 and 1783, the French Montgolfier brothers experimented with paper hot-air balloons. On September 19, 1783, they sent a sheep, a duck, and a rooster aloft at the palace of Versailles, France, in front of an amazed King Louis XVI. Two months later, on November 21, two of Louis's courtiers, Pilatre de Rozier and François Laurent, became the world's first aeronauts. They went up in a Montgolfier balloon and sailed a distance of five miles (8 km) before landing safely in a field.

What is happening?

The hair dryer blows hot air into the bag. Because hot air is less dense (lighter) than the surrounding cool air, it rises to fill the bag. Once full, the bag may float upwards because the warm air inside the balloon is lighter than the air outside. You need a lot of hot air, however, to lift even tissue paper, so this bag will not float as well as a real balloon. It may work better if you move to a cold room. If the balloon tips over sideways, add a few more paperclips to the basket to weigh it down and keep the balloon upright.

2 Glue the pieces together around the edge to make a bag, leaving a hole at one end. Make a basket as shown below. Glue thread to the edges of the basket then attach them to your balloon with paper clips.

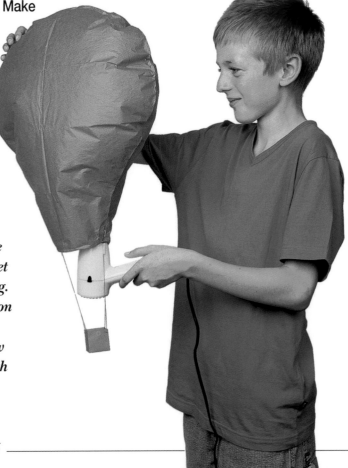

To make the basket, cut out a shape like this from thick paper; fold up along the lines; and glue the tabs to make a cube.

Hold the top of the balloon with one hand, then fit the nozzle of a hair dryer, set at "low" heat, into the open end of the bag. Switch the hair dryer on and let the balloon fill with warm air. Keep holding on until you are sure it is full of really hot air. Now try letting go of the top of the balloon. With luck, it will float upward a little. This works best on a very cold day.

HOW BIRDS FLY

Birds are perfectly made for flying, with their wings and feathers and light, hollow bones. Birds usually fly using one of two main methods: either by gliding with their wings held still or by flapping their wings up and down.

Gliding uses much less effort than flapping, and birds that are able to stay in the air a long time tend to be the best gliders. Only birds with long wings can glide well, because short wings do not give enough upward lift. Birds of prey, like kites, eagles, and falcons, are usually good gliders, hovering in the air as they search with their sharp eyes for food on the ground. So too are swifts, gulls, and gannets.

Many seabirds are good gliders because they often have to fly long distances over the ocean without a rest. Albatrosses, petrels, and shearwaters have long narrow wings that enable them to soar upward on rising currents of warm air, called thermals. Often, birds circle upward on a thermal, then glide slowly down until they find another thermal to carry them up again. In this way, they can cover huge distances without once beating

> ## Did you know?
> Most birds fly between 20 and 60 mph (30–100 km/h). But the spine-tailed swift can fly at more than 100 mph (160 km/h), and the peregrine falcon can reach an astonishing 217 mph (350 km/h) when stooping (diving on its prey).

their wings. Albatrosses are especially good at this kind of gliding—called dynamic soaring—and can keep it up for many days on end.

Most smaller birds flap their wings to fly, and even birds that mostly glide flap their wings to take off and land. Powerful muscles in the bird's breast pull its wings up and down.

For the downstroke, one set of large feathers, called primary feathers, close and push the air down and back. This thrusts the bird up and forward. For the upstroke, the primary feathers part and let air flow through as the wings gently rise, ready for another downstroke. Vultures flap slowly, while hummingbirds flap their wings so fast— sometimes more than 50 times a second—that the wings vanish into a blur.

FLYING ON WINGS

Unlike balloons, airplanes are heavier than air, but they can stay up because they have wings to support them. Wings provide the lift an airplane needs to get it into the air and to stop it from falling out of the sky.

Unlike bird and insect wings, airplane wings are completely rigid and do not flap or beat. But they work in a similar way to a bird's wing when the bird is gliding. The secret lies in the combination of the wing's movement through the air and its special shape.

A wing is not just long, thin and flat. It is very slightly arched from front to back, and it is also slightly fatter on the front or "leading" edge. If you took a slice through an airplane wing, it would look a bit like a flattened comma.

A wing shaped like this is called an aerofoil. As an aerofoil slices through the air, it makes the air flow past it in such a way that the air flow lifts up the wing.

Just how much lift the wing gives the airplane depends on the angle and shape of the wing and how fast it slips through the air. The shape of the wing is critical, and airplane makers spend a great deal of time designing it to provide just the right amount of lift.

Up to a point, the faster a plane flies or the more steeply the wing is angled, the more lift it provides. For instance, an airplane can get extra lift for climbing, by moving faster and dropping its tail end so that it cuts the air at a steeper angle.

In focus

HOW WINGS WORK

An airplane's wing is lifted by air flowing above and beneath it as it slices through the air. Because the top of the wing is curved, air pushed over the wing speeds up and stretches out. This stretching of the air reduces its pressure. Underneath the wing, the reverse happens, and pressure here rises. The result is that the wing is both sucked up from above and pushed from below.

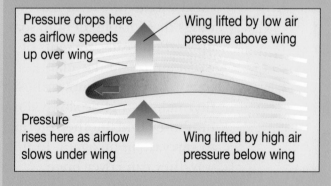

Pressure drops here as airflow speeds up over wing

Wing lifted by low air pressure above wing

Pressure rises here as airflow slows under wing

Wing lifted by high air pressure below wing

AEROFOIL

You will need

✓ Several rectangular sheets of lightweight paper

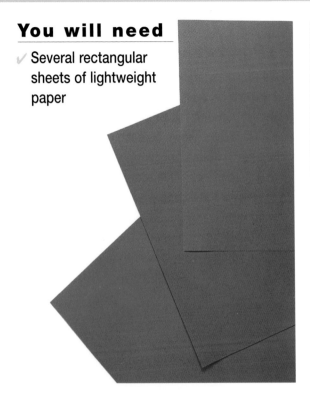

1 Hold a piece of paper vertically between your finger and thumb, then let go. It will probably drop straight to the ground.

In the real world

WING MATERIALS

The wings of the earliest airplanes were made as light as possible. Typically, they were constructed of linen stretched over a thin wooden frame and stiffened with varnish. Although such wings were light, they were fragile, which limited how fast the airplane could fly. In the 1930s, airplane engineers began to design stronger wings of light metals, such as aluminum. These allowed airplanes to fly faster using more powerful engines. The extra speed and power produced more lift, so bigger, heavier planes could be built.

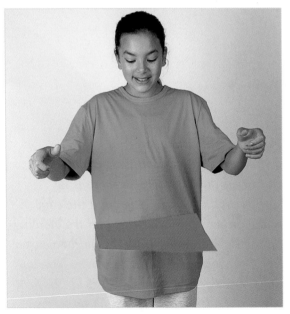

2 Now, hold the paper flat between your hands, as level as you can, then let go. It will flutter slowly to the ground.

What is happening?

All these experiments show how a wing is supported by air if it is the right shape and moves through the air in the right way. The last step shows how the real lift does not come from air pushing up the wing from underneath, but from the speeding up of air over the top. In your experiment, the wing is still, and the air is moving past it as you blow over the paper. The effect is the same when a wing moves through still air.

3 Next, grasp two corners of the paper's short edge and drag it swiftly through the air. The far end of the paper will lift.

Finally, grasp two corners of a shorter edge of the paper. Let the far end curve down loosely, so there is no stiffness in the paper. Now hold the edge of the paper up to your lips and try blowing across it. You might think it would be easier to lift the loose end of the paper by blowing underneath the paper to push it up. In fact, you will find it easier to lift the paper by blowing across the top. With practice, you should be able to get the paper to fly out almost level.

FLYING FORWARD

An airplane's wings can only lift it when they are slicing through the air. So the plane must keep moving forward. If it ever stops moving or "stalls", the wings no longer give lift and the plane drops like a stone.

An airplane can keep moving just by falling gradually forward. Airplanes called gliders fly like this. But the plane slowly loses height, which is why glider flights are short. So most airplanes have engines. Engines provide the extra "thrust" or push to keep the plane moving forward. Engines also give the power for a plane to take off by itself and fly in any direction.

Airplane engines push or pull the airplane along in one of two ways. Small, light planes usually have engines similar to automobiles. The engine turns a propeller that pulls the aircraft through the air. A propeller has angled blades that act like spinning wings, thrusting the plane forward in much the same way as wings lift it upward.

Larger aircraft and most warplanes use jet engines. Jet engines are much more powerful than propeller engines and can thrust even big airliners along at speeds up to 1,200 mph (1,900 km/h)—almost twice the speed of sound.

The simplest jet engines, called turbojets, work by pushing a jet of hot air out the back to thrust the plane forward. Air is scooped in the front and squeezed by spinning blades called compressors. The squeezed air is drawn into the middle of the engine. Here it mixes with a spray of fuel and is set alight. As the fuel and air mixture burns, it expands dramatically and bursts out the back of the engine as a high-speed jet of hot air that drives the aircraft rapidly forward.

Engines like these were used on the supersonic airliner, *Concorde,* and fast military planes. But most airliners use quieter and cheaper-to-run jet engines called turbofans. These combine the hot air jet with the backdraught from a whirling, multibladed fan to give the extra thrust needed at low speeds for take-off and ascent.

In the real world

SUPERSONIC FLIGHT

Supersonic aircraft fly faster than sound. Flying this fast, aircraft build up shock waves in the air that create a noise, or "sonic boom," that can be heard from the ground. A plane flying at the speed of sound is said to be at Mach 1. But because the speed of sound varies with height, Mach 1 is a different speed at different heights. At 40,000 feet, Mach 1 is 658 mph because the speed of sound at 40,000 feet is 658 mph. At 30,000 feet, Mach 1 is slower.

THRUST

You will need

- ✓ An empty toilet roll
- ✓ About 10 ft (3 m) of string
- ✓ Self-adhesive Velcro
- ✓ A balloon (long party balloons work best)
- ✓ Paints and a brush for decorating your train

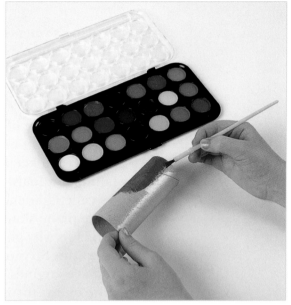

1 Paint a cardboard roll to look like a railway carriage. Stick two Velcro pads in line on the "underside" at either end.

In focus

FORCES ON AN AIRCRAFT

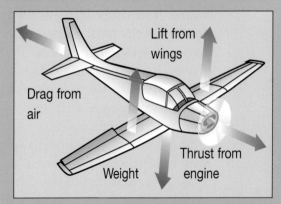

Lift from wings

Drag from air

Weight

Thrust from engine

The arrows in this picture show the direction of the four main forces acting on an aircraft: weight, lift, drag, and thrust.

Four main forces act on an aircraft when it is in the air. The aircraft's *weight* continually pulls it down toward the ground. The *lift* provided by the wings counteracts the weight and helps keep the aircraft aloft. The air around the plane rubs against it and provides a continual *drag* that holds the aircraft back. The engine (through either a propeller or a jet) provides the *thrust* to drive the plane forward, and so counteract the drag. Keeping the aircraft flying forward depends on keeping just the right balance between all of these four forces.

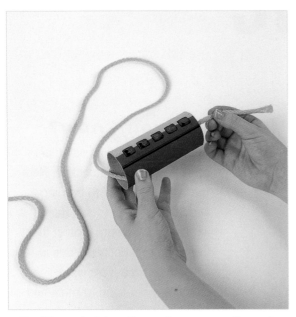

2 Thread string through your cardboard "carriage." Stretch the string across a room and secure at both ends.

3 Blow up a balloon and pinch the nozzle to keep air from escaping. With your other hand, stick on two pads of Velcro.

Keep pinching the balloon nozzle firmly. Then, using the Velcro pads, attach the balloon firmly to the underside of your cardboard carriage. Now stand clear, and let go of the balloon. Your train should shoot off up the line.

What is happening?

When you release the balloon, it quickly goes down as the stretchy rubber pushes out the air inside. As the air rushes out it collides with and pushes against the air outside.

This push is called thrust. The thrust provided by the air shooting from the balloon drives the balloon along the line. In the same way, aircraft rely on thrust to propel them through the air. A jet engine provides a similar kind of thrust, but relies on the rapid expansion of very hot gases, rather than the stretchiness of rubber.

BANKING AND DIVING

A car can only be steered to the left or right, but an airplane can go up and down as well—and also roll from side to side. This is why controlling an airplane requires a good deal of skill and coordination.

Pilots talk about three kinds of movement in an airplane: rolling, yawing, and pitching. Rolling is when the plane rolls to one side, dipping one wing or the other. Yawing is when the plane steers to the left or the right, like a car. Pitching is when the plane goes nose up or down to climb or dive.

All these moves are controlled by hinged flaps on the wings and tail. By changing the angle of these flaps, the pilot redirects the airflow and so steers the plane.

To pitch up or down, the pilot in a manually controlled airplane pulls or pushes on a control stick. This raises or lowers the elevators. To roll left, the pilot pushes the stick to the left. This raises the flap on the left wing and lowers it on the right wing. A rudder is a large vertical flap on the rear wing

Did you know?

In early planes, pilots sat in an open bay called the cockpit. Here they were exposed to howling winds, freezing cold and damp, with nothing more to protect them than a tiny windscreen. This is why most pilots wore warm clothes—wool-lined helmets and thick sheepskin coats, thick trousers and sheepskin boots.

that controls yawing. To yaw left, the pilot pushes the foot-operated rudder with his left foot, swinging the rudder left.

CONTROL SURFACES

You will need

✓ Two rectangular sheets of lightweight cardboard (each in a different color)

✓ Paper clips

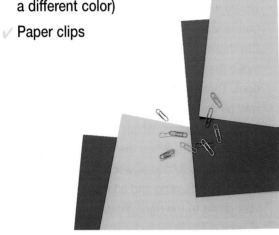

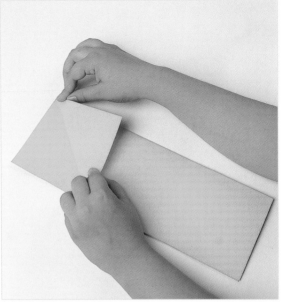

1 Fold a piece of paper in half lengthways, then make a paper airplane following the folding instructions on the left.

Making your plane

Work out your own way of folding paper to make an airplane, or follow these steps:

1. Fold paper in half then fold back a small triangle at one end of each half.

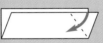

2. Fold another triangle back on each side from halfway along the top edge.

3. To make the wings, fold a triangle from halfway down the tail.

4. Open up the fold for wing triangles so they stick out at right angles.

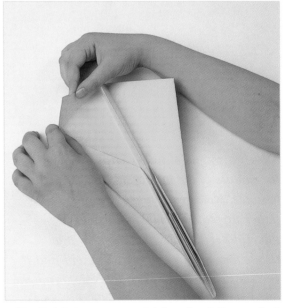

2 Fold down a small triangle at the end of the right hand wing as shown. Fold up a similar triangle on the left hand wing.

What is happening?

A well-designed ordinary paper airplane will fly straight and true for some way before veering off one way or the other. But these airplanes have extra folds that make them veer sharply to the left or the right. These folds act in exactly the same way as the ailerons (wing flaps) on a full-sized airplane, which make it roll to the left or right. When the right wing of your plane is folded upward, it reduces the lift on this wing and so makes the plane veer down to the right. When the left wing of your plane is folded upward, it reduces the lift on this wing and so makes the plane veer down to the left.

3 Now make an identical paper airplane, but reverse the flaps in step 2, with the right wing up and the left wing down.

Attach a couple of paper clips to the middle of the main fold for balance. Now grasp one of the paper airplanes firmly by the fold in the middle. Throw it as smoothly and firmly forward as you can. You will find it veers off sharply to one side. Now throw the other paper airplane in exactly the same way and in the same direction. You will find that this time it flies off in the opposite direction.

Electricity

Electricity is an amazing force. It can make lights shine and bring water to a boil. It can make the music on a CD player and create the picture in a TV tube. It can power anything from the thousands of tiny microswitches in a computer to the huge engines in a train. In fact electricity is one of the basic forces that holds every single atom in the universe together.

Electricity has been around for a very, very long time. It was formed in the first split second of the universe, more than 12 billion years ago. Yet electricity was barely noticed until little more than 200 years ago.

Newer light bulbs are efficient and use less electricity.

Did you know?

WHY IS IT CALLED ELECTRICITY?

The word "electricity" comes from the Ancient Greeks. In about 600 B.C., Greek philosopher Thales noticed that when he rubbed a kind of resin called amber with cloth, the amber attracted feathers, threads, and bits of fluff. The Greek word for amber was *elektron*. The word "electricity" was coined by William Gilbert, Queen Elizabeth I's physician (doctor). He was conducting some experiments, and he noticed that sulfur had the same power of attraction as amber when rubbed. He called this force of attraction electricity.

People had seen lightning flashing through the sky, but no-one realized that the lightning was electric. The Ancient Greeks noticed minor effects on a few tiny stones.

Important discoveries about electricity were made in the 1820s and 1830s by men such as Michael Faraday and Joseph Henry. Faraday and Henry found that electricity was closely linked to magnetism. They discovered that electricity could move magnets to make electric motors. More importantly, they found that moving magnets could generate electricity.

Once people knew how to generate electricity at will, the way was open to the modern world of electrical technology, which brought us everything from electric lights to fast and powerful computers.

By the mid-18th century, scientists had built machines that created a powerful surge of electricity by rubbing glass and sulfur together. They stored electricity in a special kind of glass jar, called a Leyden jar. The electricity could be drawn from the jar by means of a brass chain. Some scientists got nasty shocks this way!

In the real world

In 1752, American statesman and scientist Benjamin Franklin showed that lightning was electric. He flew a kite in a thunderstorm, and electricity flowed down the string as lightning flashed.

Franklin was extremely lucky to survive his experiment with electricity. Many scientists who repeated it were electrocuted. But Franklin's test kindled enormous interest in electricity, and soon scientists were discovering all kinds of things about it.

Benjamin Franklin was a respected politician, writer, and scientist.

ELECTRIC SNAKE

You will need

- ✓ metal plate or cookie tin lid
- ✓ nylon or silk scarf
- ✓ plastic pen
- ✓ tissue paper
- ✓ scissors

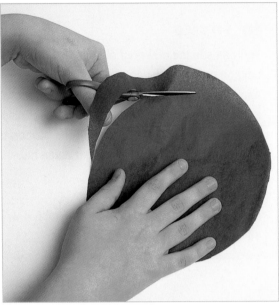

1 Cut out a disk of tissue paper 8 in (20 cm) in diameter. Use the scissors to cut the disk into a spiral about ¾ in (2 cm) wide.

In the real world

Have you ever gotten an electric shock while you are shopping? If you walk over a nylon carpet in a warm, dry atmosphere, your body can build up an electric charge. When you touch something metal, such as a clothes rack, a spark leaps from your body to the metal. You can try this at home by taking your shoes off and rubbing your bare feet on the carpet, then reaching for a door handle or metal furniture such as a filing cabinet. The electricity will leap from your body when your hand is very close to the metal object.

2 Lay the tissue on top of the plate or lid. Then rub the plastic pen vigorously with the scarf.

In focus

You can see the power of electricity by rubbing a balloon on a wool sweater. Hold the balloon against your sweater, and you can let go—it will stick in place. You can do the same by rubbing the balloon on your hair. If you lift the balloon up (like the snake spiral), you will get some hair-raising results!

If you rub a balloon against a wool vest, it will stick to your body when you let go.

What is happening?

All these effects are caused by what is called static electricity. When certain substances rub together, an electrical force called a "charge" is created between them that either attracts or repels. What happens is that minute pieces called electrons get knocked off the atoms in one substance and stick to the atoms in the other.

Substances that lose electrons are said to be positively charged; those that gain them are said to be negatively charged. Unlike charges attract each other; like charges repel.

Hold the pen over the center of the spiral snake and lift the pen slowly: the tissue will spiral upward.

FEELING POSITIVE

Queen Elizabeth I's physician William Gilbert showed that several substances possessed "electricity"—the power of attraction. In 1733, French chemist Charles Dufay discovered that the same substances also had the power of repulsion. Amber rubbed with a cloth attracts fluff and threads, but it pushes away another piece of rubbed amber. Rubbed glass will attract amber but push away fluff.

Dufay explained all this by suggesting that electricity must be two different kinds of "fluid." Put unlike kinds together and they attract each other; put like kinds together and they repel.

A balloon that has been rubbed against a cat's fur will become negatively charged. If the balloon is held near the cat, it will attract the cat's fur.

In the real world

Your clothes sometimes feel hard when they come out of the wash. This is because the fibers in certain fabrics, especially synthetics, rub together in the wash and exchange electrons. An electrical charge builds up on the fabric, making the fibers cling together so that they feel slightly stiff. Fabric conditioners in the wash lubricate the fibers and reduce the buildup of electrical charge. The fibers slide more easily over each other, and the fabric feels softer.

American statesman and scientist Benjamin Franklin thought electricity was a kind of fluid, too. But he thought there was just one fluid. When glass is rubbed, he thought, electrical fluid flows into it, making it "positively charged." "Charged" is another word for "filled." When amber is rubbed, he thought, electrical fluid flows out of it, making it "negatively charged." Whenever glass and amber come into contact, Franklin thought that fluid would flow from positive to negative until the fluids were equally balanced.

We now know that Franklin was not so far from the truth, except that it is tiny particles called electrons that are involved, not fluids (see the box). The electricity balances, or discharges, by flowing from the amber to the glass, not the other way around. When amber is rubbed with cloth, or when you rub a balloon on a sweater, electrons from the cloth rub off onto the amber or from the sweater onto the balloon. The electrons are negatively charged, so the rubbed amber and the balloon become negatively charged. The cloth and the sweater lose electrons, so they become positively charged. The difference in charge draws them together.

In focus

Everything in the universe is made up of tiny bits called atoms. Atoms are so small that two billion could fit on the period at the end of this sentence. Inside every atom there are particles called electrons. Electrons are millions of times smaller than atoms. Atoms are mostly empty space, with just a tiny core, or nucleus, in the center. The nucleus is a tight cluster of two kinds of particles called protons and neutrons. Electrons whizz around the nucleus in a series of rings. Electrons have a "negative" electrical charge and attract protons. Protons have a "positive" electrical charge and attract electrons. Neutrons have no charge. Normally, electrons are held closely to the atom by their attraction to the protons. But some outer electrons are held loosely and occasionally come away from the atom altogether. It is these loose electrons that cause the effects we know as electricity.

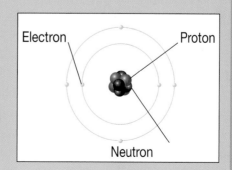

LIKE AND UNLIKE CHARGES

You will need

✓ roll of plastic electrical tape

✓ plastic mug

✓ scissors

1 Use the scissors to cut off a length of tape about 6 in (15 cm) long and stick the end of it to a plastic mug.

Now try this

Blow up a balloon and tie the end to hold the air in. Turn the cold faucet on in a large sink or bath tub to create a stream about ⅛ in (3 mm) across. When you move the balloon close to— but not touching—the water, nothing will happen. However, if you rub the balloon on your sweater several times and hold it close to the water, the water will bend toward the balloon. Rubbing the balloon makes it gain electrons from your sweater, so it becomes negatively charged. The negatively charged balloon draws the uncharged water toward it.

Holding the balloon close to the water will make the water bend toward the balloon.

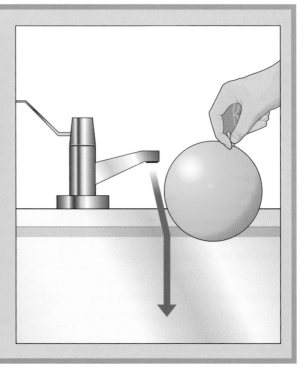

2 Cut off another 6-in (15-cm) length. Move it toward the first piece. Both pieces curl away—they repel each other.

3 Lightly stroke one piece of tape between your finger and thumb several times.

What is happening?

As each piece of tape is pulled off the roll, it pulls some electrons with it. The electrons give the tape a negative charge of electricity. Both pieces of tape have the same negative charge so they repel each other. Stroking the tape neutralizes its charge so that the unstroked, charged piece of tape is drawn toward it. A charged object is always drawn toward an uncharged object because there is a difference in charge.

Now try moving the two pieces of tape together. This time they jump toward each other. They are attracted.

ELECTRICITY IN ONE PLACE

Whenever two materials are rubbed together, tiny electrons can jump from one to the other and so create a charge of static electricity. Charges like these are being created in the world all the time. Every time you comb your hair, for instance, you are making static electricity.

Most charges are too small for you to notice anything. But static charges can also create one of the most spectacular events in nature—lightning.

Lightning is created in the same way as all static electricity: by the transfer of electrons between atoms. Thunderclouds are gigantic, and air currents tear up and down violently inside them. As they do, they sweep billions of tiny ice crystals and water droplets past each other. The crystals and droplets collide with each other and transfer electrons. The crystals take on a negative charge, and

Lightning is caused by electrons transferred between atoms.

In the real world

In the 1930s, American physicist Robert Van de Graaff invented a device now called the Van de Graaff generator. This generator creates a gigantic static charge, which is built up by rollers on a belt of special fabric. The belt carries the charge into a big metal ball where it can create spectacular effects. Small tabletop Van de Graaff generators sometimes used in schools can generate anything from 5,000 to half a million volts. When you touch them, your hair stands on end because the charge in each hair repels the charges in the other hairs. Big generators several stories high can produce many millions of volts.

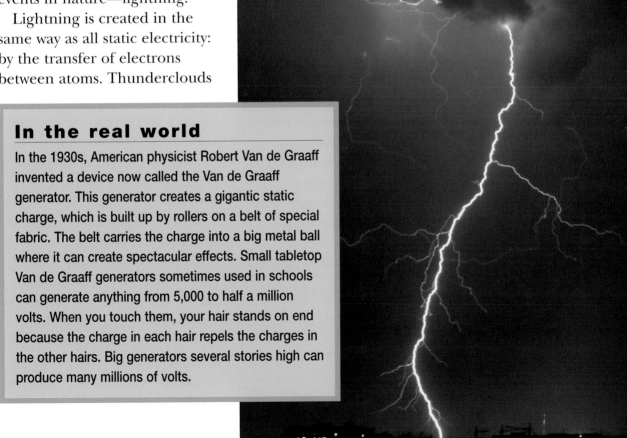

the droplets become positively charged. As the cloud builds up, the negatively charged ice crystals sink to the bottom, while the positively charged water droplets rise to the top.

Soon a huge charge difference builds up in the cloud. The base of the cloud becomes negatively charged, while the top of the cloud takes a positive charge.

Lightning flashes as the extra electrons in the base of the cloud shoot down to the ground (fork lightning) or up to the

Many buildings—especially tall ones—use special lightning rods. If these rods are struck by lightning, the electricity is guided and dispersed so that it does not cause any damage to the building.

positive cloud top (sheet lightning). This electrical discharge can be hundreds of millions of volts strong.

Obviously lightning can be dangerous. But even small static charges can cause problems. Humans cannot detect a static charge of less than 2,500 volts. When you feel a tingle as you touch a metal light switch, the current is 3,000 volts or more. Sliding across a long carpet in a centrally heated building, you can generate up to 30,000 volts.

Many computer components are designed to run at just 5 volts. So even a 10-volt static discharge could easily burn them out. This is why engineers working with electronic parts take great care to reduce static: using antistatic sprays, wearing antistatic bracelets, keeping the air moist, and so on.

A PICTURE CHARGE: XEROXING

You will need

- ✓ sheet of dark plastic (such as a plastic folder)
- ✓ old dish towel or cloth
- ✓ talcum powder
- ✓ electrical tape

1 In a place where it is safe to spill talcum powder, stick two lengths of 6 in (15 cm) of tape onto the plastic sheet.

In focus

Xerox machines create images with black toner rather than talcum powder. Inside, a roller drum coated with a light-sensitive material called selenium is given an electrical charge. A light scans across the picture to be copied and beams it onto the drum via mirrors. Selenium conducts electricity better when exposed to light, so the electric charge flows away from the picture's lighter areas and stays on the dark areas. Then negatively charged toner powder is dusted onto the drum. It sticks to the positively charged, dark areas because opposite charges attract. The drum rolls over a sheet of paper, transferring the picture to the paper.

2 Sprinkle some talcum powder onto the towel and rub it in.

What is happening?

Peeling the tape off the plastic leaves a charged area behind. This charge attracts the powder, creating an image in powder where the tape has been peeled off.

3 Hold the plastic sheet flat with one hand and carefully peel the tape away with the other hand.

4 Shake talcum powder from the towel as evenly as you can about 8 in (20 cm) above the plastic.

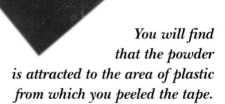

You will find that the powder is attracted to the area of plastic from which you peeled the tape.

Magnetism

Magnets come in different sizes and strengths to serve different purposes.

Did you know?

The word "magnetism" comes from the Ancient Greek city of Magnesia. It was here that a shepherd was said to have found that the iron nails in his sandals stuck to certain stones. These stones must have been made of the magnetic mineral, magnetite.

Magnetism is an invisible force that either drags things together or pushes them apart. The most familiar magnets may be the tiny decorations you stick on refrigerators. But there are many other magnets you can see around the home too, perhaps holding refrigerator or cupboard doors shut. There are also magnets you can't see, in the door bell, in telephones, televisions, and in the motors in appliances such as food mixers and electric toothbrushes.

Magnets attract some metals but not all. Materials that are affected are called magnetic materials. They include iron, nickel, cobalt, and various kinds of steel. Magnets have no effect at all on materials like copper, aluminum, concrete, and wood, which are called non-magnetic materials. Non-magnetic materials have no effect on magnetic materials either.

Some materials, such as iron and nickel only keep their magnetism when close to another magnet. These are called soft magnetic materials. Other materials, such as mixtures of iron, nickel, and cobalt, keep their magnetism permanently. These are called hard magnetic materials.

Because magnets only attract or push away certain materials, you might think that magnetism

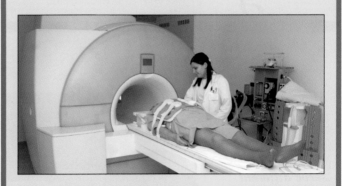

MAGNETIC IMAGING

Magnetism can help doctors see inside the body, using a system called Magnetic Resonance Imaging (MRI). For an MRI scan, the patient is surrounded by very strong magnets that pull on tiny particles, called protons, inside every atom in the body. Normally, protons point in all directions. But the magnets pull them around so that they all point the same way. A short pulse of radio waves briefly knocks them out of line again. Then, as the magnet snaps them back into line, the protons send out radio signals themselves. The system's special scanner picks up billions of these little radio signals and builds up a computerized picture from them.

is an interesting but quite limited effect. In fact, magnetism is important throughout the Universe. Magnetism combines with electricity to make a remarkable force called electromagnetism. Electromagnetism is one of the basic forces of the Universe. Electromagnetic force is at work inside every single atom, holding it together. Without this electromagnetic force, all matter would fall apart.

NATURAL MAGNETS

Some magnetic minerals, such as hematite (which is also known as haematite), are used in jewelry.

Some materials that make longlasting magnets occur naturally in the ground. The Ancient Greeks, Romans, and Chinese all knew about rare stones, called lodestones, that had the power to attract iron nails. Lodestones are magnetic because they contain a magnetic substance called magnetite. Magnetite is a black mineral found in many rocks. The world's biggest deposits are in northern Sweden. The mineral haematite is also magnetic.

Today, most magnets are made artificially. Traditionally, they were made of iron or iron

ROCK MAGNETS

Many rocks began life as molten lava from volcanoes. While the rock was still liquid, magnetic particles in them could swing around to point north, like little compasses. But, once the rock cooled and turned solid, these little magnets were frozen in place. So, if the rock ever moves, the particles move with it and no longer point north. By studying the direction of magnetic particles in ancient rocks, geologists can work out how the rocks have moved through the ages. This is called paleogeomagnetism.

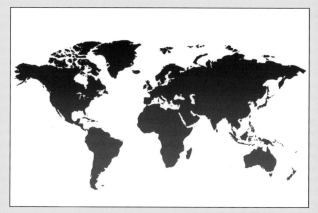

Continents move slowly over millions of years. By analyzing the directions of magnetic particles frozen in ancient rocks, geologists have been able to trace the continents' path across the world.

and nickel. These are called ferromagnets. In the 1940s, much stronger magnets were made from Alnico. Alnico is an alloy, or mixture, of the metals aluminum, nickel, and cobalt, along with iron and copper. Neither aluminum nor copper are magnetic by themselves, but in this mixture they help make powerful magnets.

Even stronger magnets were developed in the 1970s and 80s from what are called rare-earth, or Lanthanoid, elements. The best known rare-earth magnets are samarium-cobalt magnets (made from cobalt and the rare-earth samarium) and neodymium-iron-boron magnets (made from iron and boron, with the rare-earth neodymium).

CERAMIC MAGNETS

Not all magnets are solid metal. Many are made from ferrite powders. These are natural magnetic rock minerals like magnetite, made from iron oxides combined with another metal, such as nickel or strontium. To make magnets, ferrite powders are mixed into a paste, pressed into shape, and exposed to a strong magnet, to line up all the ferrite particles. The paste is then hardened by heat, like ceramic pottery in a kiln, which is why such magnets are called "ceramic" magnets. Ceramic magnets are cheap to make and can be molded into any shape, so they have a wide range of uses, such as in microphones and speakers, electric motors, and refrigerator doors. The powders can be mixed into rubber to make flexible magnets or even bonded into waferthin sheets or tape. "Stealth" planes are painted with ceramic magnetic powders to make them invisible to radar.

MAGNETIC MATERIALS

You will need

- ✔ A bar magnet
- ✔ Thin cardboard
- ✔ Paper clips
- ✔ Materials for testing, such as thumbtacks, a plastic comb, a plastic spoon, metal knives, and other small household objects

1 Touch each material with the magnet. See how many materials stick to it. Many metals do, but plastics do not.

In the real world

MAGNETIC HOME

There are magnets in many places around the home. There are magnets, too, in every electric motor, from those that turn CDs and computer discs to those that drive electric toothbrushes and food mixers. Magnets also help make the sound in the loudspeakers of sound systems such as stereos, radios, and televisions. The magnets in a loudspeaker turn an electrical signal into sound. As the signal varies, the magnets pull weakly or strongly on another magnet attached to a cone of card or plastic, making the cone vibrate. The vibrations of the cone make the sound.

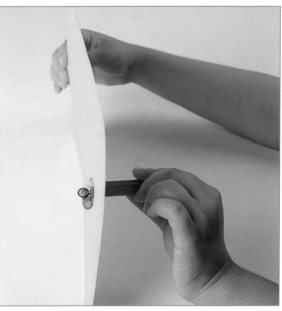

2 Many light metal objects stick so well to a magnet that you can pick them up. You may even be able to lift heavier things.

3 Magnetism is not blocked by cardboard. Hold the magnet against one side and try dragging thumbtacks up the other side.

What is happening?

The first three steps showed how certain materials are drawn to a magnet. These are called magnetic materials. The test with the line of clips shows that when these materials are stuck to a magnet, they themselves become magnets too, so that other magnetic materials stick to them.

If you pick up paper clips with a magnet, some clips are picked up even though they are only touching other clips rather than the magnet directly. Try laying out a line of clips, just slightly overlapping. Hold the magnet against one end and see how many clips you can drag along.

MAGNETIC POLES

In many magnets, the force of magnetism is especially strong at two points. Typically, these two points are at opposite ends of the magnet and are called poles.

When a magnet is hung by a thread and can rotate freely, it always ends up pointing the same way, with one end pointing to Earth's North Pole and the other to Earth's South Pole. This is because Earth is a giant magnet, and all magnets on Earth are influenced by it. The two ends of a magnet are

A compass uses the forces of Earth's magnetic poles to indicate direction such as north, south, east, or west.

called the north, or north-seeking, pole and the south, or south-seeking, pole.

If two magnets are put together, they will either snap together or spring apart. If the north pole of one magnet meets the south pole of another, the magnets will pull together. But if the north meets north or the south meets south, they will push apart. Alike poles always repel each other; unlike poles attract.

Did you know?

The Ancient Chinese knew that a magnet points north if allowed to swivel freely. As early as 2500 BC, a Chinese emperor is said to have used a lodestone, or magnetic rock, to guide his troops through thick fog to win a vital battle.

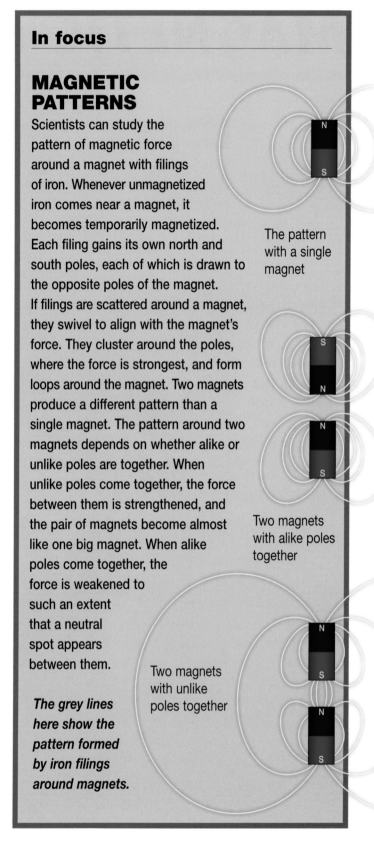

In focus

MAGNETIC PATTERNS

Scientists can study the pattern of magnetic force around a magnet with filings of iron. Whenever unmagnetized iron comes near a magnet, it becomes temporarily magnetized. Each filing gains its own north and south poles, each of which is drawn to the opposite poles of the magnet. If filings are scattered around a magnet, they swivel to align with the magnet's force. They cluster around the poles, where the force is strongest, and form loops around the magnet. Two magnets produce a different pattern than a single magnet. The pattern around two magnets depends on whether alike or unlike poles are together. When unlike poles come together, the force between them is strengthened, and the pair of magnets become almost like one big magnet. When alike poles come together, the force is weakened to such an extent that a neutral spot appears between them.

The grey lines here show the pattern formed by iron filings around magnets.

The pattern with a single magnet

Two magnets with alike poles together

Two magnets with unlike poles together

MAKING A MAGNET

You will need

- ✔ A bar magnet
- ✔ A large needle
- ✔ Metal paper clips

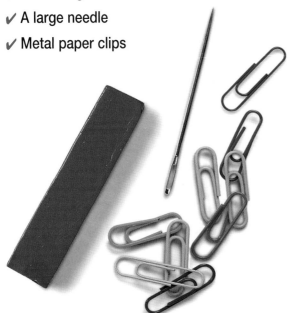

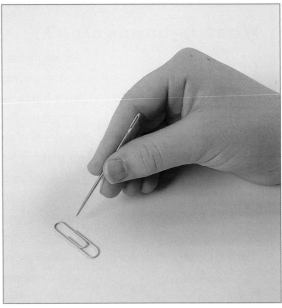

1 Make sure the needle is unmagnetized by trying to make a clip stick to it. If it is unmagnetized, the clip will not stick.

In focus

MAGNETIZATION

Unmagnetized magnetic materials can be turned into magnets in a number of ways. One way is to stroke them with another magnet, as in this experiment. Another is to hit the material with a hammer with a magnet close by. Before you begin, the magnetic domains (see "What is Happening?") point in all directions. As the material is hammered, the domains are gradually shaken into line with the magnetism of the magnet nearby. This works especially if the material is first heated, then hammered as it cools down.

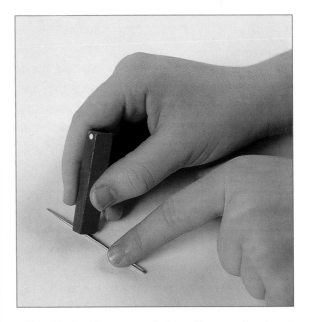

2 Stroke the magnet along the needle about 20 times in the same direction, lifting the magnet away between strokes.

What is happening?

In the unmagnetized needle, domains are aligned randomly

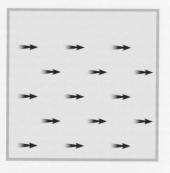

In the magnetized needle, domains align the same way

If a magnet is cut in half, the result is two new magnets, each with a north and south pole. If the pieces are cut in half again, the result is two more magnets. Indeed, no matter how many times a magnet is cut in half, right down to microscopic level, the result is always two new magnets. It is thought that all magnetic materials are made up of lots of tiny groups of atoms, called domains, and each of these is like a mini-magnet with its own north and south poles. In fact, within each domain, even the atoms themselves are like tiny magnets, with north and south poles. They are called atomic dipoles.

When the needle is unmagnetized, the poles of its domains point in various directions. Since the magnetism of each domain pulls in a different direction, the combined magnetic effect is zero. When a magnet is drawn over the needle, however, it pulls the domains so that they all point in the same direction: their magnetism is combined and the needle becomes magnetized. In steel, the domains stay lined up once they are aligned, and the steel becomes a permanent magnet.

After stroking with the magnet, the needle itself should now be magnetized. You can test its magnetism against metal objects. The needle is still quite weak compared with the original bar, but it should be strong enough to pick up a paper clip.

ELECTRICITY AND MAGNETISM

Power station generators make electric power by spinning big magnets inside a ring of electric coils. The magnets are driven around by rotating blades called turbines. In most power stations, the turbines are turned by steam heated by coal, oil, or nuclear reactions.

Did you know?

Generators in power stations push out electricity at an awesome 25,000 volts. To make it usable in homes, the current is fed through a device called a transformer. The transformer uses electromagnets to generate a much weaker current, of just over 100 volts.

Magnetism and electricity are like opposite sides of a coin. Wherever there is electricity, there is magnetism, and, wherever there is magnetism, there is electricity.

In fact, an electric current creates its own magnetism, which is not so different from the magnetism of a bar magnet. Electricity can be used to make strong magnets, called electromagnets. Unlike metal magnets, the magnetism of an electromagnet lasts only as long as the current is flowing. So, electromagnets can, literally, be switched on and switched off.

If electric wire is coiled into a loop, its magnetism becomes stronger. It gets even stronger if the wire is wound into a tight spiral. Such a spiral is called a solenoid. A rod of iron through the middle of the coil boosts the magnetic effect even more. Most electromagnets are solenoids wrapped around a core of iron.

Just as electric currents create magnetic fields, so magnets can create electric currents. If a magnet is moved near a coil of wire, an electric current is generated in the wire. Or if a wire is moved near a magnet, electricity is generated. It makes no difference whether the wire or magnet move; electricity is generated when a wire moves relative to a magnet. Scientists say the magnetism induces, or starts, a current in the wire, an effect that is called electromagnetic induction.

Nearly all our electricity is made by generators using this effect. Most generators work by spinning magnets between coils of wire. The stronger the magnet, the faster it turns, and the more coils there are, the bigger the current generated. Power stations have banks of giant generators; automobiles each have their own.

In the real world

FARADAY AND ØERSTED

The link between magnetism and electricity was first spotted in 1819 by Danish physicist Hans Øersted. Øersted saw that a magnetic compass needle swivels when it is near an electric current. About 10 years later, Michael Faraday in Britain, and Joseph Henry in America, showed that a magnet has an electrical effect too, but only if it is moving. Faraday showed this by moving an iron bar magnet in and out of a coil of wire, and by moving a loop of wire close to a magnet. A current was produced only when the bar or wire was moving.

SEEING A MAGNETIC FIELD

You will need

✔ An empty plastic soda bottle

✔ A bottle of inexpensive cooking oil

✔ A bar magnet

✔ Steel wool

✔ Scissors

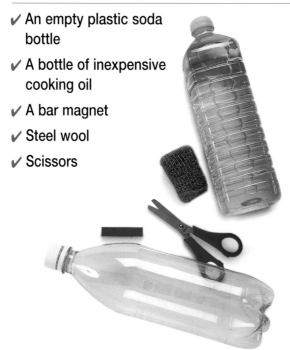

1 Cut tiny strands off the ball of steel wool and collect them in a dish. You will need about one tablespoon of clippings.

In focus

FIELD LINES

Scientists often think of magnetic fields in terms of their effect on electrically charged particles such as electrons. If a charged particle is in a magnetic field, the magnetic force will move it along a certain path. This path is called a field line. The closer together field lines are, the stronger the magnetic force. The pattern of clippings in the experiment here show the field lines around a bar magnet, and how they loop around from one pole to another. Each kind of magnet or combination of magnets has its own pattern of field lines.

2 Pour the clippings carefully into the plastic soda bottle, then pour in the cooking oil to half fill the bottle.

What is happening?

Around every magnet, there is an area where the magnet exerts its effect, called a magnetic field. The magnetic field gradually gets weaker farther from the magnet, but is very strong around the poles. In this experiment, clippings falling in the magnet's field are moved by the magnet. The pattern of clippings shows the shape of the magnet's field. The direction in which each clipping points depends on the direction of the magnetic force in that particular part of the magnetic field. You will see from this that the field curves around between the poles.

3 Screw the top firmly onto the bottle, then shake it vigorously so that the clippings mix in with the oil.

Once the clippings are mixed thoroughly in the oil, stand the bottle on a table. Now try placing the magnet vertically against the side of the bottle. You will see that the clippings in the oil close to the magnet are drawn to it immediately. After half a minute, you will see that the clippings have drifted into a pattern of curving stripes around the magnet. Shake up the bottle and hold the magnet sideways against it. Is the pattern of clippings any different? Then, try various other positions for the magnet and observe the clipping pattern that forms.

The Importance of Science Experiments

Science is about knowledge: it is concerned with knowing and trying to understand the world around us. The word comes from the Latin word, *scire*, to know.

In the early seventeenth century, the great English thinker Francis Bacon suggested that the best way to learn about the world was not simply to think about it, but to go out and look for yourself—to make observations and try things out. Ever since then, scientists have tried to approach their work with a mixture of observation and experiment. Scientists insist that an idea or theory must be tested by observation and experiment before it is widely accepted.

All the experiments in this book have been tried before, and the theories behind them are widely accepted. But that is no reason why you should accept them. Once you have done all the experiments in this book, you will know that the ideas are true not because we have told you that they are but because you have seen for yourself.

All too often in science there is an external factor interfering with the result which the scientist just has not thought of. Sometimes this can make the experiment seem to work when it has not, as well as making it fail. One scientist conducted a lot of demonstrations to show that a clever horse called Hans could count things and tap out the answer with his hoof. The horse was indeed clever, but later it was found that rather than counting, he was getting clues from tiny unconscious movements of the scientist's eyebrows.

This is why it is very important when conducting experiments to be as careful as you possibly can. The more casual you are, the more "eyebrow factors" you will let in. There will always be some things that you cannot control. But the more precise you are, the less these are likely to affect the outcome.

What went wrong?

However careful you are, your experiments may not work. If so, you should try to find out where you went wrong. Then repeat the experiment until you are absolutely sure you are doing everything right. Scientists learn as much, if not more, from experiments that go wrong as those that succeed. In 1929, Alexander Fleming discovered the first antibiotic drug, penicillin, when he noticed that a bacteria culture he was growing for an experiment had gone moldy—and that the mold seemed to kill the bacteria. A poor scientist would probably have thrown the moldy culture away. A good scientist is one who looks for alternative explanations for unexpected results.

Glossary

acceleration: A change in velocity over a period of time. It can mean either a loss or gain in speed or a change in direction, or both.

aerofoil: A wing shape that promotes lift. Typically it is curved down at the front and back and has a streamlined shape to help air flow over it easily.

atom: The smallest particle of any chemical element.

banking: When a plane steers to the left or right and leans over in the direction it is turning.

centrifugal force: The apparent outward force on an object that is turning in a circle.

charge: A quantity of electricity.

chemical energy: Energy stored within chemical bonds.

current: The flow of electrical charge produced when electrons move.

drag: The force that holds an aircraft back as it tries to fly forward. It is mainly air resistance: the friction between the plane and the air.

effort: The force applied to a machine to move a load.

electromagnet: A magnet created by passing an electric current through a wire wrapped around a core of magnetic material.

electromagnetic induction: The start of a current in a wire as a result of spinning a magnet between coils of wire.

electromagnetism: The combined effects and interaction of electricity and magnetism.

electron: A tiny particle that whizzes around the nucleus of an atom.

energy transformation: The change of energy from one form to another.

field: The area around a magnet that is affected by its magnetism.

force: Any push or pull that accelerates an object to a new velocity or changes the object's shape.

fulcrum: The point at which a lever pivots.

gravitational attraction: The pull of gravity acting between two objects; it is weakened by distance.

gravitational potential energy: Stored energy due to gravity.

inertia: The natural tendency of an object to stay still or keep moving in the same direction or speed, unless forced to accelerate. Inertia is equivalent to mass. The heavier an object, the greater its inertia, and the more force is needed to accelerate it.

ion: An atom that has a positive or negative charge.

kinetic energy: The energy due to movement.

lift: The force that lifts an aircraft up and keeps it

flying. Airplanes get their lift from the movement of the wings through the air.

load: The force resisting movement in a machine.

lodestone: Stones that are naturally magnetic because they contain the magnetic mineral magnetite.

mass: The total amount of matter in an object. The mass of an object is the same no matter what gravitational forces are affecting it.

mechanical advantage (MA): A measure of how much easier a machine makes a task. MA is the force coming out of the machine divided by the force put in.

orbital velocity: The speed a spacecraft must reach to continually orbit the earth without falling back to the ground.

pivot: The fixed point around which something turns.

pole: One of the two points on a magnet where its magnetism is strongest.

potential energy: Stored energy, ready to make something happen.

speed: The rate something is moving, measured by the distance traveled divided by the time.

static electricity: Electricity formed by a piling up of stationary charges in one place, rather than a current.

terminal velocity: The maximum speed a falling object reaches. It depends on the point where increasing air resistance meets the acceleration due to gravity.

thrust: The force pushing an aircraft forward through the air, usually provided by an engine.

turning effect: How a force acting in a straight line at one place on an object turns it if the object is held at the pivot.

universal constant: A numerical value that stays the same in every situation.

velocity: The rate something is moving in a particular direction.

weight: The force with which gravity is acting on an object. The more mass an object has, the stronger the effect of gravity on it and so the more it weighs.

work: How much something moves when energy is transferred from one place to another.

Index

Page numbers in **bold** indicate photos or illustrations.